THE HEBREW SAGA

"As a teil tree, and as an oak."

Isaiah, 6:13.

THE HEBREW SAGA

by

Gershon Rubin

Philosophical Library
New York

Library of Congress Cataloging in Publication Data

Rubin, Gershon.
    The Hebrew saga.

    1. Legends, Jewish.   2. Bible.   O.T.—Legends.
3. Tannaim—legends.   4. Rubin, Gershon.   5. Jews—Soviet
Union—Biography.   I. Title.
BM530.R78   1984   296.1'9   84-1745
ISBN 0-8022-2451-2

My first name, Gershon, is similar to the Greek word *geron* (old man). Thus, through my "geronoscope," I viewed the over-four-thousand-year-long written history of the Hebrew nation, which resulted in the origination of this my world-view, or world outlook.

G.R.

To

Ruth, Henry and Anna

Contents

Part One: In the Fascinating Luminosity
of the Lesser Light   11

Part Two: The Roll of a Book   57

Part Three: The Tanaim   179

PART ONE

In the Fascinating Luminosity of the Lesser Light

1

It was a warm, serene and moonlit summer night. Absorbed in my meditations, I sat late in the evening at an opened window of my room. Advanced age and accompanying insomnia had put me among those who rise early and sit up late. All of a sudden I remembered having read lately of one who said: "When I was young, I had been burning as a flaming fire.... But now that I am old, I am not burning any more...I smolder continuously...." I knew this saying fit me well.

Indeed, very often I had had the feeling that my thoughts were like coals which crackled, hissed and whispered endlessly in my ears, thus disturbing my peace of mind.

This happened every time I was getting ready to while away my leisure hours in philosophical meditations, a favored pastime. At such times my smoldering thoughts would throw me into a fit of melancholy, brooding over the wrongs of my life.

After many such experiences, I learned how to stave off their intrusions, how to get rid of them altogether. And so, whenever they began to disturb and interrupt my meditations, whenever they threatened to surround me like a swarm of wasps, I would plunge into reminiscences of my innocent childhood and adolescent years at the turn of the century. Once awakened and stirred, those memories rushed in and flooded my mind, and I saw myself as a young boy, a pupil of one of the Heders of the town.

It happened that I glanced at the moon, and the sight of the round and shining face evoked in me the picture of the ceremony of the blessing of the "new" moon.

I saw myself standing amid a gathering of adult bearded men with their young sons, who had just come out of the synogogue after the evening prayer. We were standing in the middle of a quiet unpaved street of a small provincial town. Together with the whole congregation I heard myself reciting: "Even as I raise myself up to you, but cannot touch you, so may my foes be unable to touch me with evil intent."[1]

While uttering those words, the adults would raise themselves up on their tiptoes, without bending the knees, which would intimate—though not too closely—the raising up toward the moon. But we, the small fry, would really jump up and down in our utmost pleasure. And in spite of the solemnity of the hour the youngsters would be ready to continue hopping, but the adults would be quick to stop us.

In those days, sons of the congregation would be put under the yoke of learning the Torah at an early age. Boys would thus be deprived of the pleasure of childhood games. They were denied every possibility of gratifying their childhood wishes. No wonder, therefore, that they jumped at every opportunity for having fun, even while reciting the prayers of the blessing of the moon, a rite performed once a month when the moon shone with the brightest luminosity.

To the youngsters' few hilarious moments of hopping fun soon would be added some joyous moments of vocal fun. When each of the adults started addressing his neighbors with "shalom aleichem," which means "peace be with you," and in return was answered "aleichem shalom," "with you be peace," all this being repeated three times in succession—then the

---

[1] From the Prayer book.

youngsters would instantly chime in, repeating these phrases again and again in our thin and mirthful voices, while broad smiles appeared on our lively faces. Actually, we youngsters turned those phrases into a sing song and would have gone on with it had not the adults been quick to stop us, as they had stopped our antics before.

I remember also how together with the congregation, I would say in a loud voice the blessing on viewing the shining moon: "Blessed be Thou, O God, our God, King of the universe, who created the heavens by His command, and all their host by the breath of His mouth. He gave them a fixed statute and season so that they should not alter their appointed charge. They are glad and rejoice to do the will of their owner. The worker of truth, whose work is true. He bade the moon renew itself, a crown of glory to those burdened from birth, who likewise are destined to renew themselves and to glorify their Creator because of the glory of His kingdom. Blessed be Thou, O God, who renews the months."[2]

The meaning of every word of that blessing was known to me because I had already spent a few years in the Heder, and the "holy language" was familiar enough to me. Besides, I had become used to the saying which instructs "that the ears should hear what the mouth pronounces." I used to do this myself when saying the prayers, which I did three times a day by heart.

And so, while I knew the meaning of every word of the blessing, I must nevertheless say that I did not yet grasp the idea, the essence of it. This I learned later, when I became more versed in Hebrew lore and was able to comprehend and cherish the spiritual and poetical riches of that wonderful prose poem expressed in a most concise language.

I remembered also how once on such a night I became transformed into a state of ecstasy by the sight of the grandeur of the skies, studded with countless stars, amid which the full

---

[2]From the Prayer book.

and shining moon reigned majestically. It seemed to me that I watched all this in a dream. My eyes became glued to the shining disk of the moon, and I looked into the face of a gigantic being whose face only could be seen, not its body. Moreover, while I stared at the moon, it also looked at me, and with every passing moment its face shone more and more upon me.

And my heart was filled with fear and at the same time with delight. I was full of anxiety lest I should become moonstruck after staring so much at the moon, but my heart was also filled with joy on viewing such a wonderful and unique vision.

The result of all this was that at the end of the ceremony the full and shining moon saw me standing all alone in the middle of the deserted street. Neither the people who left the street while, apparently, engaged in lively conversation, noticed me remaining behind, nor did I, in my fascination, notice their departure.

As soon as I had touched upon my childhood, the reminiscences of my Heder years came to life. I beheld my first year of Heder. It was one of a few Heders for beginners. A private Heder owned by a "Melamed," or teaching Rebbe, whose sacred work was to teach the five-year-old sons of the congregation the letters of the Hebrew alphabet and the spelling of non-polysyllabic words. Gradually the young pupils would be able to read the Hebrew text, vocalizing it properly and clearly. However, they had not yet been taught the meaning of the Hebrew words they were uttering.

Thus it was a mechanical reading, preparing the pupils for an advanced Heder, where they would begin to learn the Torah and become acquainted with the contents of the Book.

It would begin in a particular way. Together the young pupils would read in a loud voice the first page of Genesis word by word, and the Rebbe would immediately translate every word into the mother tongue. In this same manner the following pages would be learned, day after day, week after week for the whole first year, during which the child acquired a certain bilingual vocabulary.

A few years would elapse, and the young sons could then be heard reading parts of the Humash, or the Pentateuch, and also were able to master some of Rashi's commentaries. (Rashi was an important eleventh century commentator of the Book and the Talmud.)

Up to the age of ten or eleven, the young sons would be continually at work learning the Torah. The Humash would unravel stories of a strange world: stories of the ancient world of their forefathers Abraham, Isaac and Jacob; of the twelve tribes of Israel; of the Pharaohs and the Egyptian bondage; but above all of Moses and his actions both in Egypt and in the wilderness during the forty years of wandering from Egypt to the banks of the Jordan River.

The stories are narrated in plain and comprehensible words. Unlike the storybooks of other nations, in which lengthy narrations tell of human beings or animals performing heroic and even superhuman acts with supernatural strength or by cunning, in the Pentateuch stories only God predominates, as for instance in the case of Balaam's story. In it the ass is not depicted as a subtle animal that can speak by her own will. Of the ass it is said: "The Lord had opened her mouth, the mouth of the ass, and she said unto Balaam..."[3]

Thus God Himself participates in all the stories whether by His word, command, His strong arm or His finger. In every story God's Providence is seen and felt, and Providence makes haste to reward good deeds and punish transgressions against Him.

And so, at the Heder the young students would find their delight in the various stories of the Humash. Their shrill and loud voices would be heard outside the Heder as they repeated the portions of the Torah in their bilingual manner.

---

[3]Num. 22, 28.

When they came across a story that contained some queer and funny things their reaction would be spontaneous; their cherubic faces would brighten and on their lips would appear broad smiles.

Every once in a while it would happen that one of them could not help giggling, and in a moment he would be joined by others and instantly the whole Heder would break out into loud and boisterous laughter.

The Rebbe would make haste to show his strong hand to the frolicsome children by using the rod that was always at hand ready for action. The hardest punishment would be dealt out to those pupils whose laughter was loudest and most boisterous.

Not only was the Humash taught in the Heders. The Rebbes would also teach the Prophets and even the Katoobim, the Hagiographa. For, after a thorough study of the Humash, the young sons of the congregation were certainly able to absorb the works of the Prophets, works full of flames of fire.

And so, the Heder students at the age of eleven or twelve would be able to read any part of the Book in the usual bilingual way. And the young students would attain all that knowledge without ever being taught the grammar of the Hebrew language.

Yet, as a matter of fact, it should be stated that the constant repetition of the portions of the Book with the commentaries of Rashi made the teaching of Hebrew grammar unnecessary.

As to the language itself, it should be said that not in vain is the Hebrew language called "Lashon Kodesh," the holy tongue, since it is the language of the Scripture, the language of the Mishnah, and also of the interpretations of the Scripture.

It is also the language of the prayer books and the writings of the Hebrew scholars. One would never be allowed to use the "holy tongue" for the secular purpose of everyday conversation.

And now back to the Heder. It was unique not only because of the bilingual method by which the young pupils mastered the Hebrew language. There was something else that made it unique. The Heder was not a secular school, since every minute spent by the young students in the Heder would be wholly given to the studies of the Book. Yet neither was it a religious school. The fact is that the religious tenets and rules, all the traditional systems by which the Hebrews had lived since the destruction of the Temple by the Romans, and by which the Orthodox part of the nation lives to this day, all this would be left to the child's parents.

Moreover, it would be incumbent upon the fathers to explain to their sons the meaning of difficult words, passages and even whole portions of the prayer books—particularly of the prayer books of the High Holydays, which were full of poetical expressions and of rarely used words and sayings. Thus it should be said that the Heder was a learning place, a place for learning the Torah.

It was the first step of the young sons of the congregation on their lifetime path of seeking knowledge for its own sake; of yearning for the knowledge of the Torah which leads to the knowledge of God and His Law.

As to the Heder teachers, or Rebbes or Melamdim, they lived a pious life; they performed their sacred work faithfully and with a perfect heart. The learning in the Heders would take place in an atmosphere full of enthusiasm and diligence. This attitude the students would bring with them into the Yeshivah, a higher learning place which they would enter after spending one year in the preparatory Heder where they would encounter Talmud learning, the deep reasoning of the Gemorah.

O, the Yeshivah, the university of Hebrew lore! The Yeshivah, into which every family would yearn to send its sons to spend the adolescent years in the study of studies, in the learning of the Talmud.

The Yeshivah, where each of the sons was apt to become a Talmud Hacham, a learned man full of divine knowledge and the spirit of the Torah. The Yeshivah, where the young students would plunge into Talmudic dialectics; where they would be absorbed in the studies of the Talmud with its numerous commentaries that are full of profound reasoning. The glorious Yeshivah, from which great Rabbis would emerge to become the religious heads of congregations and their spiritual leaders.

My reminiscences now bring up the language difficulties which the students had to overcome when entering the Yeshivah. I remember that the language problem (the Gemorah, as we know, is not in Hebrew but in Aramaic) would be solved the same way the problem of the Humash Hebrew was solved. While the mastering of the "holy tongue" by six- or seven-year-old pupils would require a few years, Aramaic would be mastered by ten-eleven-year olds in a few weeks.

Besides Aramaic is linguistically and phonetically close to the Hebrew language, and every page of the Humash carried a marginal translation of the Hebrew. No doubt the closeness of the two printed texts caused the Heder pupils to become acquainted with Aramaic even before their Yeshivah studies.

And so, the students growing up, whose thin necks had been brought under the yoke of learning the Torah at the age of five, at the age of eleven and twelve were ready and willing to continue their learning in the Yeshivah. They were very naturally ready and willing to move from the easier to the harder, and the Talmud was the hardest subject of study after the study of the Scripture.

Thus the rising sons of the congregations of the Children of Israel would be fed spiritually by both the Heder and the Yeshivah. The thorough study of the Book resulted in the ennoblement of their hearts.

An old saying has it that what is first learned is best remembered. Therefore it can be stated that the sons of the congregations would forever carry the dedicated love of justice and truth which was imprinted on their tender hearts by the impressive and expressive exhortations of God's messengers. The Prophets' flaming words were absorbed by the young pupils and at the age of twelve and thirteen they were able not only to absorb the divine words, but even to moralize on them.

As to the Yeshivah, the studies of the Talmud demanded considerable mental aptitude, without which the students would be unable to grapple with the dialectics of the Gemorah, unable to grasp the debates of the Amoraim, creators of the Gemorah. These debates were based upon profound reasoning by which the Amoraim deduced unknown truth from that already made known by the Tanaim in the Mishnah. Thus the study of the Talmud would greatly sharpen the minds of the students and implant in them the love of reasoning.

I remembered that very often some students would have to give up the Yeshivah. Actually, even in the preparatory Heder a kind of a natural selection would take place. For some youngsters the learning of the Gemorah was "too wonderful; it was high, they could not attain unto it."[4] And this was because of their physical or mental condition, or both.

Such students, together with some others coming from very poor homes, would have to go into apprenticeship to learn some trade or profession. They would grow up in the congregation as laborers, as pious workers who after a hard working day would hasten to the synagogue eagerly to listen there, between the afternoon and the evening prayers, to a learned man expounding in the bilingual manner on certain ideas—either from the Aggadah, which consists of homiletic passages from the Rabbinic literature, or from the Midrash which consists of homiletic interpretations of Scripture, or from the readings for "the sayings of the Fathers" in the afternoon hours of certain Sabbath days.

Besides, there was the most cherished book of the Psalms for individual reading in every congregation of the Diaspora. It was most cherished particularly by those who were not versed enough in Hebrew lore to be able to spend the Sabbath leisure

---

[4]Ps. 139, 6.

hours over a Mishnah, over a page of the Talmud, or over the weekly portion of the Humash.

My reminiscences did not stop at that for, in connection with these Heder dropouts, my memory immediately brought up the expression "am-haaretz." It is as old as the Goluth is. It came into existence in the days of the Tanaim, the creators of the Mishnah.

Literally it means the people of the land, but in those ancient days the meaning was narrowed to the people that work the land, or the plain people of the land, the tillers of the soil.

When the Tanaim tried to put the necks of those people under the yoke of the new statutes, rules and precepts of the Mishnah, the tillers of the soil rebelled and rejected them, and the result was that a rift and a hatred developed between the erudite urbanites and the plain people of the land, the plain people of Judea.

I mention here the rift that took place more than two thousand years ago not just for the purpose of explaining how the expression "am-haaretz" became a degrading word among the generations of the Diaspora. It will be seen further that the rift signified the beginning of a new era in the vineyard of the Lord of Hosts.

My absorption in my reminiscences seemed to come to an end. I opened my eyes and glanced at the shining moon. Leisurely I stared at it for a while. My room was flooded with the moon's mysterious light, and then I noticed the open book that was lying all the time on the window sill. Automatically I went over a few lines of the page. The letters stood out clearly in the moonlight although the print was not large. The result was that this time, apparently by association, my reading brought back memories of the prayers in the moonlight, of the ceremony of the blessing of the moon.

Those memories spurred me all at once to read those pages again, right then in the luminous light of the moon. They prompted me to action. I went over to the bookcase and took out the Sidur, the prayer book, and soon found what I wanted.

I first read Psalm 148, which should be considered an introduction to the ceremonial prayers, since the psalm speaks of the sun and the moon and the Heavens of Heavens. After the psalm I read the poetical composition, printed in very large letters, which was quoted above.

I read and reread it a few times, admiring its sublime style, its succinct language, and above all the lofty idea hidden in it. What a lofty idea to compare the renewal of the moon to the renewal of the house of Israel! My mind could not depart from the inspiring composition.

Behold, my mind had been carried away by the mere sounds of the words: "...destined to renew themselves..." For what other nation on earth is like the people of Israel? Among them God's messengers, the Prophets, indefatigably cried aloud, lifting up their voices and calling on the children of Israel to rejuvenate themselves.

The renewal idea we find first in one of the psalms of the son of Jesse, when he cried out: "Create in me a clean heart, O God, and renew a right spirit within me."[5] Then one of the greatest Prophets of Israel, Ezekiel, mentioned this idea. Thus we find him, for instance, proclaiming: "A new heart also will I give you, and a new spirit will I put within you."[6]

But very soon it dawned upon me how mistaken I had been when, carried away, I hastened to juxtapose the Prophet's idea with that of the prayer book. The fact is that the Prophets of the Lord were all their lives engaged in a prolonged, bitter and mighty struggle with heathenism in Israel, and their most passionate aspirations were to cauterize with their flaming words the remembrance of the abominations in the house of Jacob. This is what Ezekiel meant when he prophesied the

[5]Ps. 51, 10.
[6]Ez. 36, 26.

renewal of the hearts and spirits of his people, while the renovation spoken of in the prayer book means that the children of Israel, who from birth are burdened with commandments, judgments, statutes and ordinances of God's Law, are destined to renew themselves in their ancient land, in Eretz Israel, in the land promised to Abraham and his seed, which is in unison with Jeremiah's entreaty: "Renew our days as of old."[7]

Waking up from my meditations, which interrupted my reminiscences and brought me back to the bitter and palpitating Goluth reality, I gladly returned to the pithy, exalting reminiscences of the Yeshivah years, full of sensations, emotions and actions that would accompany our learning hours, actions some of which were amusing, frolicsome and even mischievous. But before touching on all that, I have to say something about the nature of our Yeshivah in general.

---

[7]Lam. 5, 21.

2

Our Yeshivah was small. The students numbered thirty or forty. Actually it should have been called a preparatory or junior Yeshivah, since at the age of fifteen the students would "graduate." For further Talmudic education they had to enter the Yeshivah of either Myr or Volozhin, two small towns in our region that housed larger and famous Yeshivahs.

In comparison with those great and renowned Yeshivahs, ours was only a small local learning institution. Our pupils came from nearby villages.

The lodging and boarding of those students coming from poor homes was the concern of the charitable women of our town, who considered it their duty to provide shelter and food to them.

The boarding was arranged in the following way. The students were assigned to "eat days"—the literal translation of the two corresponding words of the mother tongue. Each of the students, upon arrival at the Yeahivah, would get a list of seven names and addresses with an additional note telling him on which day and into which home he should go to get his daily meals. It was an arrangement that worked smoothly for years.

Such was our Yeshivah, at the head of which was a renowned Talmudist—an elderly, short man, good-natured and with a sense of humor; very near-sighted and not wearing glasses.

He was inseparable from an old-fashioned tobacco pipe, the tube of which was more than a foot long and made of interlaced thin leather strips resembling the fashionable whips with which some gallant young men of the town promenaded along the streets.

We sat on both sides of two long and narrow tables, the ends of which would be put together forming a right angle. In the space between the two tables the Rebbe would sit at a small table on which the Gemorah lay, as well as the tobacco pipe.

Every day of the first four days of the week the Rebbe would expound one page of the Gemorah, and we would follow word by word in our Gemorahs laid open before us.

His clear and strong voice, in the stillness of the house, could be heard in every corner, and we became hypnotized by his enthusiasm, which seemed to revive the discourses of the Amoraim.

Because of his extreme nearsightedness, his chin would rest on the Gemorah; his eyes were glued to the text of the page. Sometimes one of the diligent students would interrupt the Rebbe's reading, asking for additional explanation of the discussed topic. The Rebbe's face would then brighten, being pleased with the student's attention to the lesson.

But sometimes the Gemorah lesson would be interrupted in a different way. All of a sudden through the open door two or three women, wailing at the top of their voices, would rush in and run the length of the Synagogue and up the steps to the ark of the scrolls of the Torah. They would beseech the Almighty in a heart-rending wail for a sick member of their family whose only hope for recovery was a miracle from Heaven.

We would remain petrified in our seats full of sad emotions, and after the women left in haste the Rebbe would tell us that we should pray for the recovery of the sick person.

Thinking of the interruptions of our Gemorah lessons brings up something else. The door would sometimes open slowly and in would come a peasant woman carrying a chicken, or a basket full of eggs, or a piece of homespun linen cloth. The Rebbe would never be surprised by the sudden appearance of this gift on his table. He was used to it, especially on the market days in our town.

The woman would ask him in the vernacular to pray for the recovery of someone very sick in her house, and the Rebbe would answer in a broken vernacular that he would do so.

I return to the Rebbe's expounding of the Gemorah. Surely, he would be very pleased whenever he observed a student's devotion to the learning of the Torah, but he knew also that among the students there were some who were inattentive to the lessons.

And remarkably, by how the students chose their seats at the tables their attitude towards the learning of the Gemorah could be seen. The less diligent, the inattentive students would choose to sit on the outer periphery of the right angle formed by the tables, farther from the Rebbe's seat and almost inaccessible to him, on very heavy benches specially built for the Synagogue.

Those benches were indeed very heavy and cumbersome, since each of them was a combination of two parallel benches standing side by side connected all along their length by a narrow and massive pyramidal structure about two feet high—a combination of two connected benches and desks slanted in opposite directions.

Not so with the diligent, attentive students. They would choose to sit on the inner periphery, closer to the Rebbe's seat and easily accessible to him, on plain light benches.

That the choosing of the seats was in accordance with the students' attitude to the learning of the Gemorah was proven by the occurrence that took place many times in my Yeshivah years.

In the middle of the lesson the Rebbe often stopped suddenly and called one of the students by name, asking him what had been said. The confused student, as usual absorbed in his thoughts, would begin saying something incoherent and totally irrelevant to the topic in question—which answer evoked laughter among the other students and aroused the Rebbe's anger.

But the guilty boy could not be reached from the back of his seat because of the massive, pyramidal structure of the bench on which he sat, and the only way to reach him was to move the table from the bench and form a passage to his seat.

I remember how the Rebbe once tried to do so, quite unsuccessfully, because in the meantime the student had managed to dive under the table, where his position was even more secure and inaccessible than before. After that the Rebbe gave up every attempt of this kind. Instead he would pour out his anger, his bitterness, at the culprit and his like in lengthy reproaches, after which he would return quietly to the interrupted lesson of the Gemorah as if nothing had happened.

Such petty and isolated incidents did not produce any bad effect on the course of our learning. In fact, we greatly advanced in the Gemorah. We learned four pages of it every week, and each Thursday would be a day of testing. In a somewhat longer than usual sitting , the head of the Yeshivah would then examine our knowledge of that portion of the Gemorah.

How to get prepared for these tests was left to our discretion. Some of the students would do it individually at home or in the Synagogue, and others would do it collectively, so to speak, in the Synagogue. I belonged to a group of eight or ten students who would return to the Synagogue every Wednesday evening after supper. Together we would thoroughly rehearse the week's lesson from beginning to end. We would spend many hours over the Gemorah in the light of a kerosene lamp, very often staying till after midnight.

Our group would occupy about half of a long, narrow table

on both sides, and one of us would take turns sitting at the head of the table.

We would all feel as one, for we were bound together by the same feelings of satisfaction and pride knowing that only we alone sat in the corner of the spacious Synagogue reviewing the pages of the Gemorah with ardent zeal. To an onlooker this was evident by the animated voices we used, by the expressions on our faces and by our gesticulations.

Yet, as I remember, we all subconsciously felt that we were on the borderline of a mystic fright. We felt that it lurked in the dark corners of the Synagogue and that it reached even the twilight zone encompassing our table. And one night, in a moment of a relative silence, all of a sudden we heard steps over our heads. We were sitting under the overhanging balcony of the women's section of the Synagogue.

The women's section consisted of the upper part of a small two-storied building attached to the rear part of the Synagogue, its floor protruding about six feet into the men's section.

And so, when we heard steps over us ominously resonate in the dead stillness of the night, the mystic fright came down upon us and over our minds.

The dead are coming! The dead! flashed in our heads, and an unimaginable horror flung us headlong into an abyss of panic. Dumbfounded and petrified in our seats, being cramped between the heavy table and benches, we instantly did just what our instincts prompted us to do. We hid our heads under the table. Only the suppleness of our young bodies enabled us to hide that way.

Of course, children would never talk to adults about the dead coming at midnight to dance in the Synagogues, but as a matter of fact we would speak of it between us, being sure in our imagination that it was so.

Who knows how all this would have ended for us that night had we not heard all of a sudden the Shamash's (the beadle's) voice: "O ye scoundrels there, why did you stop suddenly the learning of the Gemorah?"

The Shamash on that night had changed his mind without telling us anything about it. He decided that instead of going home as usual after the evening prayer, and then having to return to put out the light and lock the doors of the Synagogue, he would spend the few hours upstairs where undisturbed he could be lulled into a nap by the thin voices of our lessons the sounds of which, no doubt, were dear and pleasant to him since he was a great Talmudist.

Finally, my memory brings up an event which fortunately took place only once in my Yeshivah years. It was a shameful event, a wild prank, which explains it but does not justify it. It showed how the pent-up longing for childish frolics remained alive in us even during Yeshivah studies.

The wild outburst of frivolity, in which I also participated, stands out before my eyes in its full clarity, in its full brazeness and spontaneity, and also by the fact that the whole body of Yeshivah students were involved in it. It was an unprecedented and impudent act, since the object of our wild prank was the Rebbe, the head of the Yeshivah, and it took place in the Synagogue, which became our learning place after having graduated from the preparatory Heder.

It happened in the winter season, when the Gemorah lessons would end at the hour close to Minhah, the afternoon prayer, and people would begin to come to the Synagogue.

The Rebbe would then leave his seat and walk over to his place at the eastern wall of the Synagogue, under a wing of the ark of the scrolls of the Torah. But on that day it happened that the Rebbe's teaching ended an hour earlier than usual. So that all of a sudden we found ourselves in a curious situation: We were alone with our Rebbe, who evidently was enjoying his leisurely stroll, with the tobacco pipe in his mouth, along the aisles between the rows of the massive benches.

Left to ourselves, we started running to and fro chasing each other and not knowing what to do with ourselves. And all of a sudden we started circling round about our Rebbe, shouting and yelling at the top of our voices, pinching each other and making faces.

Then it happened that one of us could not help touching—not, God forbid, pinching—just touching the Rebbe's sleeve, and we all began to do the same and, transported with an unexplained joy, went from touching to pulling and twisting any part of the Rebbe's apparel.

Finally one of us snatched the tobacco pipe from the Rebbe's mouth, and away we went like mad hollering, skipping, hopping, jumping and circling round about the confused Rebbe, who did not lose his temper all that time, nor raise his voice.

At the beginning of our frolics, he remained standing quietly, sucking his pipe, a smile spreading on his face. After the snatching of the pipe, he still smiled but kept repeating: "Stop it, O ye scoundrels, you have had enough of it." The good-natured Rebbe knew and understood the hidden sources of our behavior. Who knows how far we might have gone in our madness had not the Shamash (the beadle of the Synagogue) appeared suddenly in the door.

Instantly we returned to reality. The Rebbe did not scold us nor rebuke us. The tobacco pipe again in his mouth, he slowly and quietly continued to stroll in the aisles as before, while the Shamash told him that he had come in haste with ready kindlings to ignite the big logs in the enormous oven because of the frosty weather.

All these remembrances passed through my mind while I sat at the window and held the Sidur, the prayer book, in my hands. I was ready to return it to the bookcase when all at once I was seized by a warm wave of emotions evoked in me by the Sidur, my most cherished companion of my pious childhood and adolescent years. My mind gladly returned to the little Synagogue, to the Shool, so-called in mother tongue, to the cozy little Shool where we would spend most of the hours of the day.

Of the four Synagogues, closely situated in the middle of our ghetto, ours was the smallest. Just across the street was a Synagogue that belonged to the Mithnagdim, (the opponents of the Hassidim), and close to it stood the biggest Synagogue in our town. It was called "the cold shool", because there was no oven to heat it in the winter season.

We did not know anything of the deep schism that had raged between the Hassidim and the Mithnagdim, nor did we feel it in the Yeshivah. The fact was that, since the strife had cooled off long ago, a peaceful coexistence had set in, with the result that the Hassidim had their Synagogues and the Mithnagdim theirs.

I still remember one thing which revealed to me the difference between the Shools. I once went with a Yeshivah colleague who belonged to a Mithnagdim Shool to say the morning prayers in his Shool, and I was surprised to discover the existence of two versions of the prayer books, Sephardic and Ashkenazi.

Our Yeshivah Synagogue was Hassidic, and every year a few members of the congregation who could afford it would travel by horse and buggy to spend a holiday with their Rabbi. I remember that on their return they would bring with them a new Hassidic Nigun (a melody, not a worded song).

Then one of the visitors, a Heder teacher or Melamed by occupation, would teach the melody to the rest of the Hassidim. This would be done at the third Sabbath meal eaten at the termination of the Sabbath (between the afternoon and the evening prayers). That meal is called "shalosh seudoth" (three meals), intimating by this that the meal concludes the three obligatory Sabbath meals.

The meal would be served in a corner of the Synagogue, and during the meals the melody would be rehearsed a few times till it could be sung collectively. Then, I remember, it would be sung aloud and emotionally at every third Sabbath meal. Thus, a new Nigun would be added to the repertoire of the Hassidic congregation.

And remarkably the young sons of the congregation would participate very little in the rehearsals, for the adults were not interested in the vocal quality of the melody but mainly in the expression of the religious emotions stirred up by it, something unknown to young children. Only full-fledged Hassidim would be able to experience it.

The collected melodies would be used on every joyous occasion. Sometimes, when commemorating an important Hassidic event, the violinist, the director of the only professional musical band in our town, would be invited to come into the Synagogue in the evening hours. There the above-mentioned conductor would first rehearse a few new melodies with the musician, and after he had mastered them there would ensue a whole evening of Hassidic music full of great spiritual pleasure and merriment.

The musician was an elderly, pious man of the Mithnagdim congregation and a good violinist. He and his band were the musical entertainers at all the wedding ceremonies in both the Hassidic and Mithnagdim congregations. They would also be invited into the houses of the Gentile neighbors on many occasions to provide musical entertainment. As to the conductor of the rehearsals of the Hassidic melodies, I remember particularly how he would be emotionally absorbed in his prayers. With the exception of the Shmoneh-Esray (the eighteen benedictions), which everybody had to say in a whisper while standing in one place, he would say the prayers loudly while pacing quickly from wall to wall along an aisle between the benches, and everybody would try not to be in his way. Or he would stand at his desk and say the prayers quakingly, with quick short motions repeated continually.

And so, I realized, my remembrances had not only revived the learning of the Torah in the Heder and the Yeshivah. They also had touched on the life of the Synagogue, the Shool, and house of worship.

I asked myself what it was in the combination of the Shool

and the Yeshivah that attracted my mind to such a degree that I could not turn away from it. Pondering this for a while, I realized that the Shool which housed our Yeshivah remained in my memory as an unforgettable, unique experience of a divine, spiritual harmony—a harmony of the Torah and the Sidoor, of learning and piety, of the mind and the heart.

The first was imparted to us by the devotions of our Rebbe, whose heartfelt desire all his life was to teach, to expound the Talmud to the young sons of the congregation; the second was inculcated in us by our parents, by our homes and by the atmosphere of the Goluth life of Israel.

Summing all this up, it should be said that the yoke of the Torah which was put on our tender necks at the age of five— that yoke was gradually destroyed, because of the spiritual harmony of our minds and hearts, so that the learning of the Torah ceased to be a yoke at all.

The learning of the Torah became an elated spiritual absorption for, after we consumed and digested the ingenious reasoning and the logical discourses of the Mishnah Tanaim and of the Gemorah Amoraim, it was in our mouth like the droppings of honeycombs, and our souls were filled with a feeling of pride and satisfaction.

In fact, we were already able to master the intricate paths of the Gemorah's dialectics with their numerous commentaries. As to our piety, the saying of the prayers, we would be introduced to them almost in our infancy, and as soon as we attained the faculty of speech we would be taught to memorize some of the shorter prayers.

During the Yeshivah years, especially after Bar-Mitzvah, when our behavior became a matter of our responsibility, we would pronounce every word of the prayers with devotion and with understanding of its meaning. Besides, no doubt the emotional praying of the Hassidim deeply impressed us also.

Thus it can be said that in the cozy little Shool the harmony of learning the Torah and of devotion to the saying of the prayers became embodied in a tangible, scheduled, daily program. Our lives became concentrated in the Shool. The day would begin and end with the prayers, while the middle of the day would be devoted to the learning of the Torah. Such was the daily schedule of the first five days of the week, while on Friday we would be left to ourselves.

On Fridays, after going to the Shool for the morning prayer, we would be busy at home helping to prepare the house and ourselves to meet the Sabbath Queen.

Every Friday we had to study at home the weekly portion of the Humash, and it would be done in a particular manner: The Hebrew text of each passage would be read, or rather sung, in accordance with the ancient Biblical musical notes with which every word is marked, while the marginal Aramaic would only be read once.

Contentedly I went to bed, knowing that my reminiscences had been elaborated upon to a full extent. But then an idea struck my mind. It told me that my remembrances illumined not only the track which I passed. They illumined something more, and before I fell asleep I knew that I had found a task for future meditations.

3

What happened next was that fresh meditations occupied my mind, and it dawned upon me that my remembrances and the experiences I went through all reflected, not only the childhood years and the adolescent period of my generation, but also the lives of the young sons of the children of Israel in all the long Diaspora years.

I knew that the scope of my reminiscences had widened and deepened to bring my mind to a broad, perceptive and comprehensive insight into our past Goluth life. An insight which tells me, first of all, that the loud, or still, but always devout voices of the young sons of the Diaspora generations, the sounds of their learning of the Torah and of their saying of the prayers—all actually sounded a Goluth anthem, which continued to hover, to echo over our dwellings.

This anthem, this sacred tune, which for almost two thousand years sounded in our ears and in our hearts, never found us slumbering; it always kept us alive and preserved our souls. It began to sound first in Babylon, in Soora and Pumpaditah, the two ancient learning places, and later in every place where a Hebrew congregation found rest.

My insight thus tells me that we never ceased being an authentic nation which always lived under the banner on which it is written: "Torah Vaavodah"—learning the Torah and serving the Lord God, Creator of the Universe, serving Him with prayers instead of serving Him with offerings since the destruction of the Temple by the Romans.

We remained an authentic nation during a long and horrible Goluth. A nation, and not a wandering religious sect that lost its national identity after the Roman victory over Judea. A nation did we remain, always devoting ourselves to our faith and in spirit never parting with the Promised Land, with Eretz Israel, being forever and ever spiritually bound together by the "Lashon Kodesh," by our holy tongue.

Behold, the prayer books, our most cherished linguistic treasure, are full of many linguistic masterpieces of reasoning together with God, as the prophet Isaiah said: "Come now and let us reason together."[1] Reasoning full of penitence, propitiations and extolling the Lord God of Israel.

The prayer books are also full of allegiance to Eretz Israel. It can be found in all the daily prayers and in the midnight prayers, which are special prayers in memory of the destruction of the Temple, and in propitiation for the restoration of Israel in the Promised Land. Jerusalem and Zion are mentioned throughout the prayers.

The prayer book was an open book to every member of the congregation and it would be an unimaginable thing to assume that a son, unless he were a deaf-mute, could grow up in his home without being sent into the Heder, thus remaining forever an illiterate member of the congregation of the children of Israel, a member unable to say the prayers.

It should be also remembered that on our banner, in addition to "Torah Vaavodah," is found the verse saying: "If I forget thee, O Jerusalem, let my right hand forget her cunning."[2]

And it could not be otherwise after the study of the Talmud

---

[1]Isa. I, 18.
[2]Ps. 137, 50.

with its commentaries. They all speak of the way of life of the ancient Hebrews in their land, in Eretz Israel, and this can be substantiated by the titles of the six orders of the Mishnah that constitute the backbone, so to say, of the Talmud. The first order is called "Seeds,"[3] the second "Feasts,"[4] the third "Wives or Women,"[5] the fourth "Nezikin" (damages or torts), the fifth "Kadoshim," (sacrifices brought to the Temple), and the sixth "Tahoroth," (cleanness or cleanliness). From all this it can be clearly seen that their contents are concerned with the holy land, with its soil and with the Temple with all the services performed therein by the Priests and the Levites.

The learning of the Torah thus kept us spiritually in Eretz Israel, in the Promised Land, in the land of Cannaan; and in that Kingdom of our souls there could be found knights, Princes and Kings.

The knights were those who all their lives remained faithful to the learning of the Torah. Whatever might have been their occupation, they would never fail to persevere in perusing a portion of one of the orders of the Mishnah, or a page of the Gemorah.

Then there were the Princes, the Matmidim (the most diligent students), who would become so engrossed in their studies that they would be apt to sit over the Gemorah day and night. In our small Yeshivah I remember one such Matmid. He would very often spend whole nights learning the Torah, taking a nap for a few hours on one of the benches before going back to the Gemorah. His face was always aflame, while his emaciated body corroborated the truth of the saying "The Torah is apt to weaken man's body."

And finally came the Kings, called Gaonim (the Geniuses of the Torah), who would find their way in the labyrinth of the

---

[3]Zroim in Hebrew.

[4]Moadim in Hebrew.

[5]Noshim in Hebrew.

Torah even with closed eyes, so to speak. Unperturbed and unconfused they would follow the mazes of the reasoning of the Amoraim, imparting and expounding to their disciples the ingenious ways of the Torah.

My insight into the spiritual world of our Goluth life filled me again with joy and pride, knowing that I had lived to participate, together with the young sons of my generations, in the realization of the divine harmony of Torah Vaavodah, and to join the chorus that would exultingly sound our sacred anthem, whose melody still echoes in all the congregations of the children of Israel.

But it saddens me to say that we were the last generation of this kind. I accentuate the words "of this kind." We were the last of those generations which, as a whole nation, all to a man, kept allegiance to the divine harmony of Torah Vaavodah.

We belonged to the last generation of this kind because we came into the world at the end of the nineteenth century. I was born in the last decade of that century, and at the age of ten I entered both the Yeshivah and the twentieth century. A century that is all discord, in which harmony is not understood. A century in which all the social, political, and religious institutions, established on earth as if forever, had been broken up, had been cracked by an irreparable ideological discord, topped with the apocalyptic split of the atom.

Yet at the beginning of this century our generation, born in an isolated region of Eastern Europe, still lived with the tradition of the olden days. The emancipation that took place earlier in Western Europe reached us only after the First World War. It arrived with horrible social upheaval, and wherever the emancipation arrived the congregations were torn apart.

My insight brought out also reminiscences about the materialistic side of Goluth life in those times. We lived in a nineteenth century ghetto, which was neither like that of the Middle Ages nor like concentrations camps of the twentieth century.

We lived in White Russia behind "a settlement line" by

which we were fenced off from the rest of the Russian Empire. Only West of that imaginary line were we permitted to settle— in any city or town, big or small, but not in the villages where the peasants lived.

We lived in accordance with our sages' saying: "...go and support yourselves by dealing with each other." We certainly lived in poverty in accordance with another saying of our sages, "...poverty agrees with the children of Israel (poverty is no disgrace)." Of great economic support would be the market days that took place once a week in our town, for while we were not allowed to live in the villages where the peasants lived, the peasants would come into the town to sell the products of their works and to buy the products of our craftmanship, or products brought from near or far by our efforts as merchants.

The economic misery of our lives would never offset the spirit and the soul. A perceptive onlooker could see and read in the eyes and on the faces of the ghetto inhabitants an expression of dreaming with open eyes; dreaming of the ecstatic bliss and joy of the holiness of the past and of the coming Sabbath days; dreaming of the sounds of learning the Torah, and above all of the "reasoning with God" in prayers. All those exalting things would occupy every minute which was free from the burden of the struggle for existence.

Besides that "settlement line" which was forced on us, there was also a spiritual line or fence established by tacit agreement between us and the Gentile environment, and in the same degree in which our culture was unwanted by them, so was their culture unwanted by us. I remember the older generation that grew up in the nineteenth century—how they lived out their lives while never being interested mentally or spiritually in anything else beside Torah Vaavodah.

Even those members of the congregation who would do business with the neighboring population would be satisfied with the possession of a limited vocabulary of the spoken vernacular.

True, it would happen that a Hebrew boy would be admitted to the secular elementary school. Yet there remained an insuperable, indisputable obstacle on the boy's path to such a school. How could a son of the congregation walk on a Sabbath morning to the school carrying books and then, sitting at the desk, do the exercises? How could he desecrate the holiness of the Sabbath by all those things?

Thus the spiritual fence remained unbroken. I remember how the sons of the older generations would grow up in the learning of the Torah till reaching the age of manhood. Usually they would continue to sit over the Gemorah till the age of eighteen, and according to the sayings of the fathers "eighteen is for marriage."

And so, they would actually "graduate" into marriage at that age. They would be given brides coming from houses which could afford to provide the young couple with housing and boarding for a few years. In those times every father would yearn to have his daughter married to a scholarly man, to a Talmud Hacham.

Some of the married scholars would sooner or later go out into the world to start their own businesses, but some would continue uninterruptedly to sit over the Talmud until they finally attained the Rabbinical Ordination, and eventually would become the religious and spiritual leaders of a congregation of the children of Israel.

I left the Yeshivah at the age of fifteen and did not go to any of the great Yeshivahs to continue the learning of the Torah. This was for many reasons, one of which was that the idea of "eating days" was not to my liking. The other reasons will be stated later.

At the age of fifteen I began to earn my own living by teaching others the knowledge of the Torah I acquired in the Heders and the Yeshivah during the ten years I studied there.

Thus I became one of the tutors sought by the isolated Hebrew families which, after moving from the town ghetto, went to dwell in the big estates which belonged to the mighty landlords of those times. Such families would be permitted to dwell on the borders of the estates as lessees of dairies, of water or steam flour mills, and also as leaseholders of alembics situated in the middle of the woods.

The leaseholders of the alembics would possess the exclusive rights of digging up in a given portion of the forest all the stumps with their long and thick roots that remained in the ground after the gigantic pines had been sold to and cut down by timber merchants. From the dug-up roots turpentine, tar and coal then would be produced.

There were also some families who did business on a small scale as wood merchants. Such families would be also allowed to live in the countryside, close to the estates' managing offices. All those families were well off in comparison to the ghetto inhabitants.

In addition, there were some other families which would leave the town to make a living in the countryside, but they would move not into the estates. They would move into the villages. Such families would be granted permission to live among the peasants because the village inhabitants needed the services of the trades of those families.

Thus, in every big village lived two or three Hebrew families: a blacksmith, a tailor and a keeper of a small store where the peasants could buy necessary articles. But very seldom would there be found in the villages a cobbler or a shoemaker, since in those times the peasants' footwear would be old shoes worn over wraps or rags.

All those Hebrew families, from the first day of their settling outside the towns, would be burdened with the problem of their children's education, and the problem would be solved by bringing over from a town a hired Hebrew tutor. The hiring would be made on a half yearly basis: from Passover till Rosh-Hashanah and from the first week after the feast of the Tabernacles till Passover.

Now, as a beginner, and mainly because of my young age, I

could not expect to get a teaching post in any of the homes of the above mentioned families. If, as I have said before, I did become a tutor at the age of fifteen, it happened because I took advantage of a fair opportunity.

In a village ten miles away from my hometown lived my uncle, my mother's brother. He was a blacksmith, and he lived there with his big family of grown-up and small children. At the end of the feast of the Tabernacles I went to that village to teach my cousins the Torah. I was hired to tutor them during the fall and winter months of 1905-1906, at the end of which I was to be remunerated with thirty-five rubles.

They lived in a house similar to all the other houses of the village, which were lined up on both sides of an unpaved road about a mile long. The houses had thatched, low roofs. The uncle's house consisted of two parts under one roof.

An entrance led into the larger part of the house. It had no ceiling and no windows, it served as a barn and pantry. From it a door led into the smaller, habitable part of the house. It consisted of one room, of about twenty-five by twenty-five feet with a low ceiling and a stomped, earthen floor.

A large Russian oven occupied about a quarter of the room, and in the opposite corner was a large bed under which chickens were kept in the winter season. The space between the other two corners belonged to us, to the young generation.

In the bright corner, between two windows, a table was placed round which I and my cousins would spend, every day except Friday, about eight hours in zealous study of the Torah.

I remember how my aunt would sit for hours not far from our table doing her knitting and listening to our thin, loud, and animated voices with a blissful expression on her face. She understood the meaning of the words because of the bilingual method of our learning. From time to time she would even ask questions about some of the Biblical personages, the names of whom were familiar to her.

At night the table would be removed and our half of the

house turned into an improvised bedroom where all the available benches were put together. It was a big family, harmoniously knit together.

Everybody busied himself with some work. The older sons would spend the whole week, till Friday afternoon, outside their home. Their profession was making shingles by hand.

The demand for shingles would come from the farmstead owners. Those farmers were expected by the Tsar's government to become the forerunners of a planned reform that would change and improve the social, economic, and political conditions of the lives of the peasants who for ages had lived in abject poverty and despair, remaining illiterate and neglected.

For this purpose the government began to encourage and materially help those of the peasants who were willing and ready to give up their parts in the collective ownership of the village land, and to settle outside the village where each would possess individually a parcel of land on which to build his own farmstead.

Those well-to-do farmers preferred shingle roofs to the thatched ones, and for this purpose they kept large quantities of aspen logs as raw material for shingles. Thus my three cousins were busy continually, and when they would return home for the Sabbath day our improvised bedroom would be somewhat crowded. But "crowdedness—and no offense," as a Russian saying has it.

On weekdays, before starting his work at the smithy, my uncle would manage to say the morning prayers while we were still asleep. As to us, the aunt would see to it that we did not fail to say the prayers in time, before having breakfast.

Every Sabbath morning—rain, snow or shine—unless there was a blizzard, my uncle, donning his overcoat over the Talith, would walk to the neighboring village where a Minyan (ten men) would gather together to conduct the traditional Sabbath morning services in the house of one of the participants living there.

The following years I had no difficulty finding a tutoring post with one of the families that resided on the premises of the estates, and every half-year I would change the location, being eager to meet more people and enjoy diverse views of nature.

Looking retrospectively at those isolated, scattered Hebrew families, I perceive them as sturdy, exotic and insoluble particles of a whole, of a nation, whole in body and soul, insoluble in the human ocean.

From my personal point of view, when looking retrospectively at my adolescent years which I spent in the bosom of nature, in the bosom of the pristine nature of those times, while living near the plain people, the plain toilers of the soil of whom it was written and spoken openly among the intelligentsia of those days that their lives actually manifested a continuous seeking of God and His truth—when delving so amongst my reminiscences of those years, I know that my world-view had been formed then, to which I remained faithful all my life, even to this day, a world-view the main components of which are love of nature and love of ingenuousness in human life.

Moreover, I also know that my world-view is in full accordance with the ideas, sensations, and emotions imbibed by me during the long years of intensive studies of the Torah, of the cherished divine Book which my hands never relinquished.

Concerning love of nature, I should say it is one of my innate properties. Since the age of nine or ten—together with other kids of that age, like a flock of birds—I would rush out into the streets in the early hours of Sabbath afternoon, into the full power of the summer sunshine, darting through the blocks of the Gentiles' section to the wooden gate that marked the town's border.

Only our racing speed would save us from the fangs of the vicious dogs which were lying in wait for us in every courtyard. In a flash we were over the gate and in the open of the fields.

Hurriedly we passed by enormous beds of growing vegetables of every kind. We all were very excited and joyfully happy.

Our senses eagerly absorbed the surrounding phenomena of nature.

We heard the larks singing in the skies, the buzzing, humming and droning of the big flies and bees in the air, the chirping of the grasshoppers, the bleating and lowing sounds coming from pastures not far away; we smelled the fragrance that overflowed in the air; we saw the flitting butterflies and a diverse range of colors in the bright sunshine.

We walked around delighted, touching whatever pleased us but never plucking or picking anything because of the Sabbath.

Soon, at our feet there were many small meadows which invited us to play games, to do some tumbling, or just to stretch out on the soft grass and watch nature's life around us. But in our innermost hearts we knew that our most desired aim was to reach the woods that seemed to be not that far away at the end of the fields.

After a few excursions we learned how deceitful could be a distance measured by the eye, and therefore on the following excursions we would quicken our pace and even do some running on our way to the woods. Eventually we found ourselves under the swaying crowns of the pines.

Exhausted and breathless, we threw ourselves on the ground, blissfully inhaling the fresh and fragrant air. For a while fear overtook us, remembering that we were in the woods all by ourselves, and thoughts of wolves, ruffians, and brigands flashed through our minds. But those thoughts instantly disappeared, melting away before the onrushing ideas of our forthcoming frolics.

We hollered at the top of our voices while enjoying the echoing sounds coming from afar; we sped along between the trees; we wrestled. We also paid much attention to the display of the natural signs of life around us; we followed the laboring ants carrying their loads to the anthill; we followed the flight of birds and were happy to see some vanish in a nest. In such cases we got excited discussing the possibility of climbing up the tree, not with some malicious intentions—far from it—but just to have a good look at the inside of the nest.

Such were our short stays in the bosom of nature. Short stays in which all the enchanting new sensations, ideas, and emotions stirred up in us would be mixed from the very beginning with some sort of anxiety. When darting into the street after our parents retired for a prolonged rest following a hefty Sabbath meal, we would feel some uneasiness lest we should be unexpectedly called back to do some perusings from "the sayings of the fathers." When speeding through the Gentiles' section we would be full of fear lest the vicious dogs should attack us.

Finally, when in the woods we would fear lest we should fail to return in time for the afternoon prayer. Yet it should be said that because of the fears and anxieties our elated emotions and feelings grew stronger, deeper and more impressive with every subsequent excursion.

4

After a few years of hard work I saved some money that enabled me to take private lessons in Russian for the purpose of catching up eventually with the curricula of the high schools. Such students were called "externs," their aim being to pass one day the state exams for obtaining the matriculation certificate. They then hoped, under the mercies of the quota, to be admitted into one of the eleven universities of Russia.

The "externism" flared up among us in the first decade of our century as a result of the "enlightenment" movement that struck strong roots in the hearts and minds of our young generations.

The movement attracted a great number of the Yeshivah students, stirring up in them a longing for secular education, for the acquisition of Russian culture and through it of European culture also.

The quiet ghettoes awoke all of a sudden not only to the energetic calls of the "enlightenment" movement, which was being propagated everywhere, but also to the calls of the many political, revolutionary factions which sprung up in Russia after the unfortunate war against Japan, factions propagating liberty and equality.

No wonder, therefore, that after we were graduated from our

small Yeshivah many of us did not enter the great Yeshivahs to continue the learning of the Torah.

It did not mean, of course, that the Yeshivahs had been deserted—far from it! The fact is that our sacred anthem is heard to this day—and will till the end of days—in the learning places of every Hebrew congregation in the world, and that Yeshivah students nowadays experience and enjoy the elated and blissful emotions evoked by the divine harmony of Torah Vaavodah, just as we did in our times.

After my reminiscences had been totally exhausted, I had no intention whatsoever of absorbing myself in remembering the horrors of the twentieth century from which I had tried to hide myself. I turned away and tried not to think of them.

Intuitively I stretched out my hands and grasped convulsively the Book and the open Sidur. The Book and the Sidur, the two pillars of Torah Vaavodah. The Sidur was still lying open to the blessings of the renewed moon, and again I saw before my eyes the large print of that poetic composition. And when I went over it again, an idea flashed through my mind.

I realized that the short, lofty, and inspired composition, which I shall call "The Lunar Poem," tells us of the beginning of the world and of the end of its days. As it has been stated here before, the words "destined to renew themselves" carry the meaning of the restoration of Israel in his old land, in Eretz Israel, in the Promised Land, that shall take place in the end of the days.

Thus the poem prompted me to start a scrutinizing, perceptive, and comprehensive study of the book of Genesis, from first to last line, in the hope of attaining through it some understanding about the prophesied events that will come to pass in the end of the days.

I went on reading till I reached the passage which says: "...and the Lord said: 'I will destroy man, whom I have created from the face of the earth, both man and beast and the creeping things and the fowl of the air, for it repented me that I have created them,"[1] And a picture of a terrible tragedy was presented to my mind.

All of the tragedy is related in one hundred forty-five passages. A tragedy of a world that was destroyed in its infancy, so to speak, since it had existed during only ten generations.

I read the reason why it repented Him that He had created them, namely: "And God saw the wickedness of man was great in the earth, and that the whole imagination of the thoughts of his heart was only evil continually."[2]

At this point my mind was diverted from the fact of the tragedy to the origin of its cause, to the beginning of Evil on earth, to Adam's first sin, called "the Original Sin," the credit for which goes to the subtle serpent which was more subtle than any beast of the earth being full of cunning as a pomegranate is full of seed. For this sin Adam and Eve had been justly punished.

Scrutinizing every passage I discovered that the awful curses that came down on the heads of Adam and Eve did not include their expulsion from the Garden of Eden, and the following two sentences suggest that tranquility had been set in the Garden of Eden: "And Adam called his wife's name Eve, because she was the mother of all living. Unto Adam also and to his wife did the Lord God make coats of skins—and clothed them."[3]

However, in close succession come three passages that tell us the story, the very sad story, of the expulsion of Adam and Eve from the Garden of Eden: "And the Lord God said: Behold, the man is become as one of us to know good and evil, and now lest he put forth his hand and take also the tree of life and eat, and live forever. Therefore the Lord God sent him forth from the Garden of Eden to till the ground from where he was taken. So

---

[1]Gen. 6, 7.

[2]Gen. 6, 5.

[3]Gen. 3, 20, 21.

he drove out the man, and he placed at the East of the Garden of Eden Cherubims and a flaming sword, which turned every way, to keep the way of the tree of life."[4]

Certainly it could be expected of man, who had been disobedient to God's commandment not to eat of the tree of knowledge of good and evil, that he would try also to eat of the tree of life and thus brazenly challenge the Creator's judgment of man's mortality.

So man was driven out of the Garden of Eden, and he went from bad to worse when in his offspring, in man's firstborn, Evil sprung up forcefully and blossomed with such a venom that it succeeded in instigating Cain to kill his own brother Abel, whose blood cried unto God from the ground.

Thus, Adam's house began its life with a double sin: the transgression against God and the sin against its own flesh and blood; a sin which permeated the lives of ten generations to such a degree that the Creator decided to destroy man from the face of the earth.

From that nebulous, somber and awful sight of the flooded earth my mind returned to the beginning of the tragedy of the antediluvian world, to the day when man had been driven out of the Garden of Eden, and instantly, in a flash, I discovered a bright consoling point. Although shamefully driven out of the Garden of Eden, man nevertheless was not deprived of his knowledge of good and evil, but he went forth into the open world with this divine attribute to remain in his possession forever and ever.

Did not the earth rejoice at the sight of Noah and his house, in whom not only had the knowledge of good and evil been preserved, but in whom also Good had prevailed over Evil?

Delighted did my mind cling to the sublime words of the Creator: "Behold, man is become as one of us to know good and evil..." Exalted, I reiterated the Psalmist's words: "...for

---

[4]Gen. 3, 22, 23, 24.

thou hast made him a little lower than the Angels and hast crowned him with glory and honor."[5]

At the same time I was struck with awe to realize how far we mortals are from understanding the nature or effectiveness of the Lord God's knowledge of good and evil, because it belongs to the secret things which are unattainable by us.

Not so with man's knowledge of good and evil. It lies open before us and is revealed to us by its effectiveness in our lives, in our words, and in our thoughts. It is revealed to us continually, and particularly so when our knowledge of good and evil is turned into good or evil actions.

Thus my thoughts had been diverted from the tragedy of the antediluvian world. I felt relaxed, I was soothed, I was lulled by the idea, by the lofty idea, that man possesses a knowledge of divine origin.

Almost in a drowsy condition I continued to whisper: "...as one of us...as one of us...to know good and evil...good and evil..." And my euphoric mind clung to the fact that, of all the living beings created together with man on the sixth day of the Creation, only man had attained the knowledge of good and evil. Man only, and no other living being on earth, is to possess it...only man...only...

The expression "only" electrified me. Instantly my relaxation, my drowsiness came to an abrupt end. I jumped to my feet repeating loudly: "Only...only...only..." Feverishly I turned over a few pages of Adam's chapter and read the above-mentioned quotation: "...and God saw that the wickedness of man was great in the earth, and that the whole imagination of the thoughts of his heart was ONLY evil continually."

So this is what the ten generations of Adam's offspring did with the knowledge of good and evil, they turned it into evil only, which resulted in the effacing of the image in which man had been created. But if Adam's world was a world of only evil,

---

[5]Ps. 8, 5.

it means also that it was a Demoniac world, since ONLY EVIL is the domain of Satan.

I became utterly confused, and my mind was flooded with various questions. Nay, it was hit by a volley of agonizing questions as a result of the collision of the two "onlys," and they finally crystallized in the following question: "How and when did the 'only evil' strike roots—and the strongest roots—in Adam's world?"

Surely, the answer offered itself instantly: Cain was the one whose actions were only evil. It was Cain that turned murderer, perpetrating the heinous crime of slaying his own brother. Even Cain's great-great-great-grandson Lamech was a killer, as it is written: "...ye wives of Lamech, hearken unto my speech, for I have slain a man for my wounding and a young man (a child) for my hurt."[6]

Cain's utterances in answer to the Lord God's question—they also contain only evil. In short, it is clear that Cain was the embodiment of EVIL, the source of only evil in Adam's house, which gives a full answer to the question when but not to the question how? How did it happen that the first human offspring was totally won over by Evil?

Now, Cain was not the only offspring of Adam and Eve. From Genesis we know that during his long life Adam begot sons and daughters. Furthermore, in the detailed genealogy of the ten generations neither Cain nor his offspring are mentioned, which suggests that his generations came to an end with Lamech, the killer.

Thus the same question should be applied to the ten generations, namely: How did it happen that in the offspring of Seth and his son Enoch, in whose days "...man began to call upon the name of the Lord,"[7] that in their seed EVIL became so deep-rooted as to rule relentlessly over ten generations in

---

[6] Gen. 8, 23.
[7] Gen. 4, 26.

which only one soul, Enoch, evinced a gleam of good and walked with God? But lo, happen it did, and the ten generations actually lived in a triple sin: The whole imagination of their hearts being ONLY evil, as has been mentioned here before; their hands preoccupied with continuous violence, and all flesh perverting his way on earth—as it is written: "...and God looked upon the earth, and behold, it was corrupt, for all flesh corrupted his way on earth. The earth was corrupt before God, and the earth was filled with violence."[8]

Such is the picture of the antediluvian world in which EVIL succeeded in plunging man into the depths of sin. Just think of man's full corruption, as if he never possessed the knowledge of good and evil!

Finally, I felt that I was not only confused by the tantalizing and unanswered question, but also utterly exhausted. I threw myself into a chair, facing the open window and the shining full moon, the light of which flooded my room with a fascinating, enigmatic luminosity.

My eyes became glued to the shining moon, and so were my thoughts, and I began to feel relaxed and at ease. My thoughts concentrated on the nightly queen of the skies, and this time not because "it is bidden to renew itself to those burdened from birth," but because I felt my mind become suddenly focused on the moon's natural functions in the skies.

A captivating idea flashed through my mind, telling me that the lesser light was created not only to give light upon the earth, but also for the rule of the night, and that this means that the moon is in the skies to watch eternally what is going on in the earth under the cover of darkness.

Moving round about the earth in the serene nightly skies since the Creation, it beholds and watches all the doings of the sons of men, both the good and evil doings. The secrets she keeps surely could not be told nor numbered.

---

[8]Gen. 6, 11-13.

It seemed to me that all my doubts and agonizing questions, all my thoughts, left me to soar up into the skies to present themselves to the "crown of glory," which certainly saw and watched, not only how the ten generations of the antediluvian world filled the earth with violence and how all flesh perverted his way upon the earth, but also all the vile and wily stratagems by means of which EVIL succeeded in defiling Adam's world and causing its destruction.

I became drowsy while feeling that I was hypnotized by the enchanting, luminous light. Yet, in this soporific condition, my thoughts expanded and were filled with imaginary new ideas and sensations. Surely the "crown of glory" knew of some Satanic, heinous event which occurred in the lives of Adam and Eve during their sojourn in the Garden of Eden—an abhorrent event which quickened their expulsion from the Garden of Eden lest their firstborn, their son Cain, should be born therein. So, I should beseech the "crown of glory" to share with me the mysteries of the lives of Adam and Eve, and also of the ten generations after them which lived in a threefold sin.

My imagination assured me that the nightly queen of the skies would deign to reveal to me the abhorrent ugliness of the antediluvian world for which every living substance was destroyed.

The long stare wearied my eyes, and when I closed them I knew that instead of going to bed I should slumber away the rest of the night in the chair.

Shivering, I woke up at daybreak, for a cold breeze was blowing through the open windows. I left my chair, closed the windows, and started pacing the floor in silence. I felt that the heavy burden of the tormenting deliberations had been lifted from me.

I was in high spirits for, while I was slumbering in the chair, being muffled in the bewitching, mysterious and mesmerizing light of the moon, the "crown of glory" condescended to unfold before my eyes a roll of a book, communicating to me the secrets of the antediluvian world.

Using the prophet's words, I will say that "...I did eat the roll and filled my bowels with it, and it was in my mouth as honey for sweetness."[9] Moreover, I knew also that in addition to it a thread was put into my hands which would guide me in the paths of the postdiluvian world, of Noah's world, in which we live now.

Painstakingly I will write down the vision, and shall try to make it plain—"that he may run that readeth it."[10]

---

[9]Ez. 3, 3. (In the Masoretic translation "roll" reads as "scroll.")
[10]Hab. 2, 2.

PART TWO

The Roll of a Book

5

"Thus the heavens and the earth were finished and all the host of them."[1] All was finished in six days. Only on the fifth day did various forms of life begin to come into existence. And they were completed on the sixth day by the creation of two human souls, of Adam and Eve.

And behold, on the fifth day SATAN, called Adversary by way of eminence, did not fail to come to see God's works on earth, to see the newly created forms of life on which in the course of time he would practice his wily and evil designs.

He came not alone; he was accompanied by the Angels who joined him in his defection, in his turning away from the divine knowledge of GOOD and EVIL to choose the knowledge of ONLY evil instead. Those angels consisted of demons and devils; Satan and his entourage being "the other camp."

Great was their wondering when they beheld the creation "...of the great whales and of every living creature that moveth, which the waters brought forth abundantly after their kind, and every winged fowl after its kind."[2] But the greatest surprise awaited them on the sixth day when, after creating the beasts, the cattle, and everything that creeps upon the earth, "God

---

[1]Gen. 2, I.
[2]Gen. I, 21.

created man in his own image, in the image of God created He him; male and female created He them."[3]

They saw it and wondered, and more than that. Soon they became very troubled and fear took hold of them, for they heard the blessings which the Creator bestowed on man, namely: "...be fruitful and multiply and replenish the earth and subdue it and have dominion over the fish of the sea and over the fowl of the air and over every living thing that moveth upon the earth."[4]

Deeply troubled, the demons and the devils looked to Satan for some reassuring words, and he did not tarry to remove their fears. He told them not to fear, and that neither should they be terrified by all what they saw and heard. He continued even more convincingly to tell them that "inasmuch as we belong neither to the things created on the fifth day nor to the things created on the sixth day, man shall never have dominion over us. On the contrary, sooner or later we shall subdue man and rule over him."

He thus relieved their anxiety, and the demons seemed to lose their interest in the human beings, yet very soon Satan himself was shocked and thrown into confusion, all because of the Garden of Eden.

Behold, the seventh day passed. The seventh day, on which the Creator ended His work. The Adversary saw how everything was set up on earth, how everything was established there as if in wait for his works on earth, but then he saw the Lord God again at work.

He saw how the Creator planted a Garden eastward in Eden, in which the Lord God made grow every tree that is pleasant to the sight and good for food. He also saw the river that went through Eden to water the Garden.

He saw all that, and it never occurred to him that the Garden

---

[3]Gen. I, 27.
[4]Gen. I, 28.

was planted for the two newly created human beings. So he watched the planting of the Garden with very little interest, since his thoughts were always focused, not on harmonious, creative works, but only on destruction, on the ruin that results in abomination or desolation.

His mind was already preoccupied with the vile design of finding a way to change the instincts of all the living things created on the fifth and the sixth days of the Creation: how to change all the herbivorous creatures into carnivorous, how to accustom them to the taste of flesh and blood, how to inure them to rapacity, how to wean them from the fruit of the tree and from every green herb given them for food.

Such thoughts crowded his mind, and it was therefore no wonder that the spectacle of Adam being taken and put in the Garden of Eden greatly shocked the Adversary; nay, it struck him dumb, for the spectacle told him that this was directed against him and against his camp.

He knew that the purpose of putting man in the Garden was to isolate him from the outer world lest he should fall prey to evil influences, lest he should become an easy prey to the demons and devils. Otherwise Adam would remain living among all the other living beings created together with him on the sixth day of the Creation.

All this flashed through his mind while watching how Adam was taken and placed in the Garden of Eden. Reluctantly he allowed himself to think of the heavenly wisdom by which, as he certainly knew, were wrought all the works that passed before his eyes.

Now, what is known of the heavenly wisdom comes from the description presented in the following awe-inspiring verses: "The Lord possessed me in the beginning of His way, before His works of old. I was set up from everlasting, from the beginning, or ever the earth was. When there were no depths, I was brought forth; when there were no fountains abounding with water; before the mountains were settled, before the hills was I brought forth. While as yet He had not made the earth, nor the open places, nor the highest part of the dust of the world. When He prepared the Heavens, I was there; when He set a circle upon the face of the depth; when He established the clouds above; when He strengthened the fountains of the deep; when He gave to the sea the decree that the waters should not pass His commandment; when he appointed the foundations of the earth, then I was by Him as one brought up with Him; and I was daily His delight, rejoicing always before Him. Rejoicing in the habitable part of His earth, and my delights were with the sons of men."[5]

To complete this description it should be added that the words "as one brought up with Him" are the translation of the Hebrew word "amoon," and that ancient Hebrew sages, by transposing the vowels, changed the reading of the word to "ooman" so that the phrase reads as follows: "...I was by Him as a divine tool," as an instrument of all His harmonious works. Such comment is sustained by the passage which says: "The Lord by wisdom had founded the earth, by understanding had He established the heavens."[6]

The Adversary rejected all that since he had defected from the "council of the Lord,"[7] and since he had chosen vileness to become his tool for the perpetration of ONLY evil on earth.

Satan became outraged when he saw Adam and Eve being put in the Garden of Eden to tend and to keep it, because it meant to him that they would remain forever inaccessible to him.

Yet soon he was relieved of his anxiety, and he recovered his high spirits when he heard God's words to Adam: "...but of the tree of knowledge of good and evil thou shalt not eat of it, for in the day that thou eatest thereof, thou shalt surely die."[8]

---

[5]Pr. 8, 22, 32.

[6]Prov. 3, 19.

[7]Jer. 23, 18.

[8]Gen. 2, 17.

At those words Satan perceived that a wide field of action was laid open to designs on earth which would be carried out by his demons and devils.

Watching Adam and Eve continually, the Adversary soon discovered that the tree of knowledge of good and evil became the object of Eve's curiosity. He saw how many times she would cast curious and desirous glances at the tree, and the devil-serpent was quick to creep into the Garden and beguile the woman. Surely, the other camp greatly rejoiced at their success, but it was not enough for them.

In his diabolical frenzy the Adversary embarked on plotting a new heinous design that would result in the total ruin of the world.

Obstinate and presumptuous, he did not take into consideration the fact that, among the awful curses which came down on the two human souls, were also some consoling words mercifully and graciously inserted by the Creator, words saying: "...in sorrow (in pain) thou shalt bring forth children."[9]

The words suggest that human life shall never cease on earth, but shall flow for ever from generation to generation, "...like a spring of water, whose waters fail not."[10] That man will continue to live in his seed, in his offspring begotten by him and brought forth into the world by his wife.

To all this Satan did not pay any attention. Instead, he chose to hold to his occupation, to his vocation since he had defected from God's Council. He would continue constantly, relentlessly and persistently to lead man into temptation, being confident that it would cause evil to prevail over good. He would continue to do so till the end of the days, which in his interpretation means till the ruinous end of the world. Classical examples of Satanic temptations can be found in the first two chapters of the Book of Job.

---

[9]Gen. 3, 16.
[10]Isa. 58, II.

Thus the Adversary was ready to lead into temptation both Adam and Eve. He was ready to arouse in them a feeling of discontent, bitterness, and despair because they had been so severely punished for their sin. And they began to hear voices reaching their ears in the wind of the night, voices calling them to eat of the fruit of the tree of life and bring to nought the curse of mortality, voices telling them not to be afraid to do so since the Creator had never commanded them not to eat of it.

The enticing voices finally prompted them to action, to find the location of the tree of life and to eat of it.

So they were driven out of the Garden of Eden, lest they should commit the most awful, heinous, blasphemous, and inconceivable sin under the sun. Yet their rebellious mood remained unchanged, and their hearts were neither broken nor contrite.

To the contrary, the Adversary succeeded in turning their discontent into an open revolt against the Creator, spurring Adam and Eve to force their way back into the Garden and to the tree of life, so that the Lord "placed at the East of the Garden of Eden Cherubims and a flaming sword," as has been cited here before.

The tragic result of all this was that of Cain it could be said: "...he was shapen in iniquity, and in sin did his mother conceive him."[11] And the evil, rebellious instigations continued to flow continuously into Adam's house, into his seed, into the hearts of his sons and daughters. The evil, rebellious temptations continued to take root in Adam's generations, and it seemed that evil penetrated so deeply as to permeate even their genes, with the result of turning the antediluvian world into an irreparable world of ONLY evil.

Watching continuously over the lives of Adam's generations, the vainglorious head of the "other camp" became sure of his full victory over man and that as a result the earth would

---

[11] Ps. 51, 5.

fall into his hands. He expected this to happen in one of Adam's generations.

In Enoch's days it seemed to him that his expectations were going to be materialized. He perceived this from the fact that "...Enoch was not, for God took him;"[12] which meant to him that God took Enoch lest he should perish in the imminent ruin of Adam's world. However, nothing happened, to the Adversary's great disappointment.

When Noah, who walked with God as his great-grandfather Enoch did, arrived, Satan's spirits soared up again. He hoped that Noah would also be taken by God, after which the world would be destroyed, and thus the remembrance of the human race would be blotted out from the face of the earth.

This time he was more than disappointed. He was shocked, he was dumbfounded, when he heard God's words to Noah and his sons, from which he realized that Lamech's son was to become the progenitor of a new world. He would have been even more amazed and horrified had he considered the works of the heavenly wisdom in Adam's world.

Behold, the heavenly wisdom did not forsake man, created in God's image and after His likeness. The heavenly wisdom hastened to counteract the invasion of the evil genes. For this purpose the heavenly wisdom summoned the sons of God, as it is written: "...the sons of God saw the daughters of men that they were fair, and they took them wives of all which they chose."[13] It is also written: "...the sons of God came in unto the daughters of men, and they bore children to them; the same became mighty men, which were of old—men of renown."[14] And those sons of God did not tarry to come to the rescue of the sons of men and their world.

Thus the evil defilement that penetrated into the innermost

---

[12]Gen. 5, 24.

[13]Gen. 6, 2.

[14]Gen. 6, 4.

parts of human nature initiated a war of genes, so to speak, between the human race and the "other camp," a war that went on for ten generations. Like a plague did the evil genes defile and corrupt every flesh upon the earth.

Of course, it was not a war full of bloodshed and cruelties; it was a cleansing action done by the sons of God, and only in Noah's house did their counteraction come to a victorious end. And the just and upright Noah came as a witness against the Adversary, and as a sign of the invincibility of man's purified flesh which, once cleansed from the Satanic filth, shall forever remain immune from becoming again ONLY evil.

And so, an end came to the antediluvian world, in which seemingly the heavenly wisdom could not find delight with the sons of men. Yet the words "...and my delights are with the sons of men" also pertained to the heavenly wisdom. Therefore, while the sinful world perished, there still remained a few human souls worthy of becoming the objects of the heavenly wisdom's delights, and also of becoming the originators of the postdiluvian world.

Actually, the heavenly wisdom's intentions were to keep the first human generations in the Garden of Eden under her tutalage, with the purpose of enlightening and preparing them for the fulfillment of the task assigned to them, to make man understand that the earth was to become an arena on which a constant battle would rage between him and "the other camp" of the fallen Angels with Satan at its head.

An arena on which the sons of men would always be exposed to the influences of both the Adversary's evil advice and temptations and the heavenly wisdom's good advice. The decisive choice between good and evil would belong only to man; neither by Satan nor by the heavenly wisdom would man ever be forced to make his choice.

All this means that the antediluvian world might have been the world of good and evil, but Satan was quick to overturn the tables. He was quick to turn Adam's world into an evil, spiritless mass of corrupted and perverted flesh that had to be destroyed.

Yet in spite of the horrible cataclysm caused by the vile and wily defected Angel, the heavenly wisdom did not make war against him with the intention of either destroying him altogether or forcing him into repentance by inflicting heavy punishments upon him. As is written: "...the ways of wisdom are ways of pleasantness, and all her paths are peace."[15]

And this can be corroborated by the above-mentioned two chapters of the Book of Job; in all their contents no trace at all of enmity to Satan can be found, nor any reproach or rebuke at all.

Behold, the heavenly wisdom was ready to call him to come and reason together, while trying to make him ponder and weigh his defection, his turning away from the High Council, trying also to persuade him to consider the gravity of his steps for the furtherance of ONLY evil on earth.

But the heavenly wisdom knew his obstinacy and obduracy, which makes him impervious to words and reasoning. She[16] knew that there is only one means by which she will succeed in opening his eyes and making him perceive the reality of his status in man's world.

Now, from the beginning the heavenly wisdom knew that she would not content herself with the creation of the new planet solely for the purpose of providing an abode for the defected Angel and his camp. Had it been so, she would have ended her works in two or three days; but she continued to create more and more living beings, and finished her works on the sixth day with the creation of man in His image and after His likeness.

The heavenly wisdom wrought all that with the purpose of subjecting the Adversary to a trial by setting before him a

---

[15]Prov. 3, 17.

[16]The Hebrew word for "wisdom" is feminine, and the pronoun is also feminine.

challenger. The challenger would be the newly created human being, the mortal creature made of dust of the ground, into whom the Creator breathed the breath of life.

The mortal being would possess two spiritual properties which would set him on a par with his demoniac foe, namely the knowledge of good and evil and his free will to choose between good and evil.

The heavenly wisdom knew that man would not fail to fulfill what she wished, and that he would prosper whereto she sent him and that he would accomplish her goal on earth, her goal being the utter defeat of Satan by man. And the mighty Adversary would realize that the hated and disdained creature had gone on fighting against the head of the other camp—and prevailed when Noah's house was the first to triumph over evil.

Thus, instead of the antediluvian world, the postdiluvian would become the arena of the battle between man and Satan. The obdurate Adversary, as usual, paid no attention to the heavenly wisdom's intentions and works in man's world. The fact that man was designated as his challenger did not impress him at all; it only increased his hatred against man.

The heavenly wisdom was also watching Adam's generations, but unlike the Adversary, who always looked for the imminent ruin of the world, the heavenly wisdom, on the contrary, looked for signs of GOOD in man's life. In Enoch she saw the first breakthrough against evil, the first spark of GOOD, an inextinguishable spark that shone out in Noah and turned him into a just and upright man who walked with God.

The corrupted way of life of his generations was so abhorrent to Noah that it could not lead him into temptation. Moreover, the just and upright Noah was abhorred by his generations, as it is written: "An unjust man is an abomination to the just, and he that is upright in the way—is an abomination to the wicked."[17]

---

[17]Prov. 29, 27.

When the heavenly wisdom saw all that, she finally knew that she had found rest in Noah's house, in which she would find her delights with the sons of men. And when the Creator said to Noah: "The end of all flesh is come before me...And behold, I will destroy them with the earth,"[18] the heavenly wisdom filled Noah and his sons with the Spirit of God in wisdom and understanding, and in knowledge of all manner of workmanship in wood that was necessary for the building of the Ark.

Thus, Noah and his house stepped into the new world with two virtues: the virtue of walking with God and the virtue of forming and establishing the first human social cell on earth; a cell that was to become the basis of man's life in the world in which we live now.

During their long stay in the Ark the heavenly wisdom continued to enlighten them, to prepare Noah and his house for their new life in the postdiluvian world, a world that would be quite different from the antediluvian world, which was a world of ONLY evil.

Moreover, they had enough time, while in the Ark, to ponder and digest what the heavenly wisdom revealed to them, so that they would be able to comprehend God's words to them, and more than that, would be ready and willing to obey God's commandments.

That they had been enlightened could be seen from the fact that, as soon as they went forth from the Ark, Noah built an altar unto the Lord and offered burnt offerings on the altar.

---

[18]Gen. 6, 13.

6

Inspired and instructed by the heavenly wisdom, Noah and his house perceived the differences between the two worlds. Above all it seemed to them that in the antediluvian world there existed two different kinds of human beings. One kind knew only GOOD, while the other knew only EVIL.

Not so in the postdiluvian world, in which there would be ONE Mankind, one kind of human being, in whose hearts both GOOD and EVIL would struggle together continually till the end of the days, when GOOD would prevail over EVIL and man would triumph over Satan.

Moreover, Noah and his house were enlightened to understand that in the postdiluvian world the fate of the world was put in man's own hands, that in the postdiluvian world man would judge himself and recompense himself while cleansing himself from his evil doings.

All this they learned from God's words, said to them after they went forth from the Ark: "...and surely your blood of your lives will I require; at the hand of every beast will I require it, and at the hand of man; at the hand of every man's brother will I require the life of man. Whoso sheddeth man's blood—by man shall his blood be shed, for in the image of God made He man."[1] These two sentences disclose the basis upon which the postdiluvian world was founded.

Now, the first passage serves as a preamble to the second

---

[1]Gen. 9, 5, 6.

passage, which contains the commandment, the one commandment only with which the Creator inaugurated the postdiluvian world and with which Noah and his sons were introduced to their new life on earth.

The two passages speak so much of God's loving-kindness and of His merciful concern that man should live out his years naturally and never succumb to a violent death, whether by beast or by man, and that man's life is the most sacred and most precious thing in the world.

And so, God's commandment metes out the just recompense for the most horrible evil that can be perpetrated on earth. And behold, the execution is to be carried out by man himself, as it is written: "...by man shall his blood be shed."

Thus, a sword was put into man's hand for the sole purpose of putting away the source of evil from human life, the evil of wars and bloodshed, lest it should accumulate and spread all over the world and man would have then to purify himself in a most painful and tragic way from the defiling, ruinous, Satanic evil.

A corroboration of this can be found in the following passage: "...and the Lord said in His heart, I will not again curse the ground any more for man's sake, though the imagination of man's heart is evil from his youth; neither will I again smite any more everything living, as I have done."[2] This means that when the good earth no longer would be able to bear man's corruption and violence, man would have to mete out to himself the just recompense.

An intimation of this can be also found in another passage that contains the Lord God's words: "My Spirit shall not always strive with man, for that he also is flesh."[3] This passage in its turn suggests that only the antediluvian world was to be judged by the Spirit of God, since a world in which "every flesh

---

[2]Gen. 8, 21.
[3]Gen. 6, 3.

corrupted his way on earth," such a world of ONLY evil, could never be judged by man.

These words were heard in Adam's world before it had been destroyed. And surely by God's Spirit it had been judged, and by the command of God's Spirit "...all the fountains of the great deep were broken up, and the floodgates of heaven were opened, and the rain was upon the earth forty days and forty nights."[4]

The heavenly wisdom continued to watch Noah's activity in the new world and she saw that, since God's commandment sounded in Noah's ears, his mind had become tense and alert, for he knew that the Lord God had appointed him to be judge and executor in man's world. He stiffened with authority, being ready to do his duty should such a necessity arise.

Noah was full of understanding and the knowledge that God's finger could be seen in the fact that His commandment had been put between the blessings. Which means that if man disobeys and resorts to violence and bloodshed, then the blessings will turn into a curse, because children will grow up to be slain in the blood of their youth in endless and cruel wars.

Beholding all the things that moved, crept on the earth, or in the water, and also the winged fowl of the air, Noah knew that in his new world they would be "meat for the sons of men, as the green herb and the fruit of the tree."[5]

And it happened one day, when Noah and his household were enjoying their meal, consisting not only of vegetables and fruits but also of the meat of a slaughtered animal, that Noah was led into temptation: he was enticed to think of the produce of the vine; to think that it would be good to have it added to such a meal.

When the Adversary became aware of what was going on in Noah's mind, he jumped at it. He decided he would try to

---

[4]Gen. 7, 11, 12.
[5]Gen. 9, 3.

kindle that temptation and to inveigle the just and upright Noah, to lure him into his net.

In his presumptuousness Satan was confident that a successful temptation would lead Noah and his sons to Cain's action, particularly so since Noah was also a husbandman.

For this purpose he began in every diabolical way to set before Noah's eyes mirages of vineyards full of grapevines laden with clusters of succulent grapes; and wherever Noah would walk such a vineyard would loom before him. For a time Noah was uncertain, but finally, recognizing his new status in the postdiluvian world—as judge and executor of his own judgment—he determined to challenge the product of the vine of his vineyard.

And so, Noah planted a vineyard, and he drank of the product of the vine. He enjoyed greatly the gladness it brings to man's heart, but he should have stopped short before the GOOD of the product of the vine turned into the EVIL of intoxication.

Now, it is written: "And Noah the husbandman began and planted a vineyard. And he drank of the wine and was drunken; and he was uncovered in his tent....And Noah awoke from his wine, and knew what his younger son had done unto him. And he said: Cursed the Canaan; a servant of servants shall he be unto his brethren."[6]

The word "began" is the translation of the Hebrew word "vayohel," which also has the meaning of "trembled."[7] And Noah surely did tremble with both fear and excitement while

---

[6]Gen. 9, 20, 21, 24, 25.

[7]Author's note: The word "vayohel" is a verbal form of the past tense of each of two Hebrew roots, which differ from each other by their spellings and meanings. One is a transitive verb and has a meaning of "to begin"; the other is intransitive and has the meaning of "to tremble". Whenever "vayohel" in the meaning of "he began" is mentioned in the Scripture, it is followed by an infinitive verb as the object. In our passage "vayohel" is not followed by an

embarking on a new kind of activity which he had never experienced in the antediluvian world and which he knew would lead him to challenge Evil openly.

He trembled at the contest with the lithe vine, the pernicious works of which Noah had seen many times while watching the prolonged revelries of his generation—monstrous revelries which made him shudder each time he remembered them.

Behold, Noah was not a fighter. Facing the pressing, menacing and abhorrent way of life of his utterly corrupted and perverted generation, Noah always tried to keep away from it, shunning its company.

Moreover, it can be said that while his generation lived by an ONLY EVIL instinct of life, Noah on the contrary lived by an ONLY GOOD instinct of life. So that Noah walked with God, as the sunflower walks with the sun. Such was Noah, the just and upright man in his generation.

Noah's defeat in his duel with the supple vine did not turn into Satan's victory over man. Actually, in his obdurate wantonness the Adversary imagined that Noah would invite his sons to the revelry, and when they were drunk, a brawl would ensue that would turn into a fight, resulting in bloodshed—to his utmost pleasure.

But Noah did not further Satan's design. Noah did not invite anybody of his household to share with him the product of the vine. And when he felt himself becoming inebriated, he quietly lay down to sleep off the intoxication. The only thing Satan had gained from Noah's duel with the vine was Noah's evil curse that came down on the head of the innocent Canaan. And when Noah's wrath calmed down and he was able to ponder his mishap with the product of the grapevine he learned something to remember, namely, evil generates evil.

As to the Adversary, he was upset by the failure of his design, but he did not linger on it. His diabolical mind was already

---

infinitive verb, but by a verbal form which is also of the past tense, and therefore its meaning is "he trembled."

preoccupied with a new scheme against man—with a new plan to meet the changed conditions of man's life in the postdiluvian world, a world in which man was to become his own judge and recompenser.

The blessings bestowed upon Noah and his sons were familiar to him. He remembered them from the days of Adam and Eve, but he was astonished to hear the commandment "by man shall his blood be shed." He knew that all this was the work of the divine wisdom, whose aim was to bring to nought his efforts to inure man to bloodshed.

The heavenly wisdom was delighted to see how Noah defied evil, how he initiated man's path in life, a path on which the sons of men would gradually become hardened by their constant fight against evil, which would result in their full victory over evil while putting it away forever from among their midst.

The heavenly wisdom was delighted to see how Noah thus asserted the status of the postdiluvian world as being not a world of ONLY evil, but of good AND evil, in accordance with God's words said after the flood, as it is written: "...for the imagination of man's heart is evil from his youth."[8] And in these words the expression ONLY was omitted.

As to the Adversary, he would not even try to understand the purpose of the heavenly wisdom's works on earth. He became very busy with a new plan, for a new idea flashed through his diabolical mind. It soon expanded, deepened, and turned into a grandiose scheme, into a sinister plot pernicious to man's life—nay, to man's existence on earth.

Satan was quick to learn that man's life in the postdiluvian world would hinge on the Lord God's commandment: "...by man shall his blood be shed." He knew also that Adam's world hinged on God's commandment of "...the tree of knowledge of good and evil thou shalt not eat, for in the day that thou eatest thereof thou shalt surely die."

So, the Adversary was sure that, as he had succeeded in

---

[8]Gen. 8, 21.

beguiling and inducing Eve to do what the Creator commanded not to do, so would he succeed in inducing man NOT TO DO what God commanded TO DO.

The haughty Adversary was already carried away by his wily and vile plot which was meant to result in the total destruction of the postdiluvian world. It was a far-reaching scheme embracing the whole world.

True, he knew that the first generations after Noah would surely observe God's commandment. The fact is that violence is never mentioned in the description of the generations between Noah and Abraham, the son of Terah. Of Nimrod, the son of Cush and the grandson of Ham, is written: "...he began to be a mighty one in the earth. He was a mighty hunter before God; wherefore it is said: 'even as Nimrod the mighty hunter before the Lord'."[9] So the mighty man was only a mighty hunter before the Lord, and not with a single word is violence or bloodshed ascribed to him.

There was no violence because the sword given to Noah and his sons was to become an instrument of averting, uprooting, and cutting off any attempt to commit the most heinous crime in man's world, the crime of shedding man's blood. It was to become a warning and threatening sign, the fear of which would always be before the sons of men so that they would sin not.

Yet Satan soon succeeded in obfuscating the minds of the sons of men, turning them away from the Lord God, Creator of the Universe.

Thus, paganism would be the beginning of Satan's plot; a beginning that would be followed by a more decisive step of putting in the hands of the pagan sons of men a sharpened and furbished sword. "The sword will be sharpened to make a sore slaughter and furbished—that it may glitter."[10]

---

[9]Gen. 10, 8, 9.
[10]Ezek. 21, 10.

The result would be that from generation to generation the sons of men would be inured to bloodshed, and finally would become entangled in such a complex of bloodshed as to be unable to discern between the guilty slayers and the avenger-executors or the recompensers.

The Adversary knew also that the swords' action could accomplish only a small part of his all-embracing scheme. It had to be carried out with the help of the demons and devils, and he assembled them with the purpose of setting before them the particulars of his grandiose plot.

He began with the story of the tree of knowledge of good and evil, and he clung to that subject throughout his harangue. He told them how the tree that was "a stumbling block and an offense of heart"[11] to Adam and Eve—how the Lord God's hand came down upon it, when the earth was stricken with a curse which said: "...cursed is the ground for thy sake."[12] How a violent storm sprung up carrying in its wings a scorching wind while the words of the curse were still echoing in the air.

How the earth fainted while listening to the frightening curse and the ground's moisture almost fled; how the majesty of its plants and the splendor of their blooming—the signs of its primeval, pristine vigor—all the earth's vegetative glory withered away. How every bud dried up and every flower faded, for the scorching wind consumed them unsparingly. How the era of the earth's fabulous flora was over and gone and its bareness was uncovered.

How, in additon to all that, even springs of water turned into flint, and the earth was covered with every kind of herb, densely interspersed with thistles and thorns which were to become the food of all the living things that existed on the earth.

And the tree, which Eve "saw to be good for food, a delight

---

[11] I Sam. 25, 3.
[12] Gen. 3, 17.

to the eyes and desired to make one wise"—how that tree also was doomed to destruction, which happened when a most violent blast of the wind uprooted the tree and hurled it far away from the Garden of Eden.

How the place where the tree landed turned instantly into a wilderness. How the tree did not remain there long, how the Adversary ordered the demons and devils to make haste and bring the tree to him with the roots intact, after which it was planted at the entrance into a cave. Also how he ordered them to take good care of the tree, lest it should wither, for he knew that the tree was to become the tool of the implementation of his design on earth.

He continued to tell them they should know and remember one thing: the grandiose plan would never be carried out by means of the sword only. Surely the sons of men would continusually make wars against each other, and human blood would always flow like water. Yet even the most bloody slaughters caused by the voracious sword would not result in the total ruin of the postdiluvian world.

He added that, since in the postdiluvian world man was to become his own judge and recompenser, the unusual destructive forces would have to be conceived by man's own mind and constructed with his own hands.

The Adversary pointed at the tree of knowledge of good and evil and exclaimed that this tree would provide man with unseen and unheard of forces capable of destroying all his world.

He continued his speech, saying that, since Eve's eyes saw "the tree to be desired to make one wise" such desire would remain forever in the hearts of her seed and thus man, because of his thirst for more and more knowledge, would begin to inquire and explore his world in both its depth and in its height, with the result that, being carried away by his ingenious discoveries, man would begin to pry and delve into the roots of nature and of nature's basic elements.

And one day it would come to pass that man would cross the Rubicon, so to speak, when, in his covetousness of being wise, he would venture to open the hellish firegates of heaven and nature.

At this point the Adversary raised his voice and emphatically addressed the demons and devils, saying: "You should know that after man succeeds in penetrating most audaciously into the innermost recesses of nature, there will be established a kind of harmonious cooperation between our camp and that of the sons of men. They will continue to enjoy the sweet and good fruits of the tree, while we will continue to lead them into temptation. We shall continually try to entice them, and they will be enticed; we shall continually try to induce them, and they will be induced, with the result that their sweet inventions shall turn sour and their good inventions shall turn most evil, for even their most outstanding invention, by means of which man could turn the whole earth into a sheer paradise, that same invention will be immediately turned by him into the most horrendous, most monstrous instrument of destruction—nay, of wiping out altogether life on earth; of burning to ashes everything under the sun."[13]

Thus the Adversary finished his speech; a vehement and venomous oration. A gruesome picture of man's future was presented to the cheering demons and devils. But it shall not stand, nor shall it come to pass, for all his words are ill-founded boastings.

The heavenly wisdom certainly was aware of Satan's intentions and of his works in the days to come. The heavenly wisdom knew that he would succeed in persuading the sons of men to live in idolatry. A veil of darkness would spread over

---

[13]It should be said that all this is in accordance with Shakespeare's memorable and prophetic words which say: "We but teach bloody instructions, which being taught return to plague the inventor."

man's world, and idols would be found in every corner of the habitations of the sons of men.

The heavenly wisdom knew also that all this would happen because man would forget his Creator and, cleaving to evil, man would put his trust in the idols. And in his folly he would even make his sons to pass through fire as sacrifices to the abominations.

Thus the Adversary intended to establish his kingdom on earth on two diabolical foundations, on heathenism and on bloodshed, and in his obduracy and obstinacy he was confident in his ability to inure the sons of men to endless wars, interrupted from time to time by short and illusory times of peace. It was as if the expression "war and peace" had been added to the divine words of the passage which says: "While the earth remaineth, seedtime and harvest, and cold and heat, and summer and winter, and day and night shall not cease."[14]

Yet the heavenly wisdom would not rend the mountains into pieces and hurl the rocks against him. Neither would she send out fiery arrows against him, but she would counteract his machinations in her peaceful way.

The heavenly wisdom's reaction came when her voice was heard at the end of the ten generations that passed between Noah and the son of Terah, telling Abraham the Hebrew, who was to become the forefather of the Hebrew nation: "Get thee out of thy country, and from thy kindred, and from thy father's house unto a land that I will show thee. And I will make of thee a great nation, and thou shalt be a blessing."[15]

Certainly, the heavenly wisdom would plant a vineyard in a very fruitful hill, but not before "she will make a wall about it, gather the stones thereof, and build a tower in the midst of it, and plant it with the choicest vine."[16]

---

[14]Gen. 8, 22.

[15]Gen. 12, 1, 2.

[16]Isa. 5, 2.

Thus a whole nation would arise in the postdiluvian world on which the Spirit of the Lord would rest, the spirit of wisdom and understanding, the spirit of seeking God, of seeking the knowledge of God.

Such a nation would arise for a sign, for a wonder to the world, and for a witness against evil; it would be to the world for an everlasting sign that would not be cut off, because in that nation, in the vineyard of the Lord of hosts, the pillars of idolatry and bloodshed would be smashed in the sight of all the peoples of the world.

And so the heavenly wisdom laughed and held Satan in derision knowing that, whatever would happen in the last days, it would never be the materialization of his plot, but only man's own cleansing action when man will judge himself and will mete out the recompense for all the evil he had perpetrated in the past from generation to generation.

The roll of the book ends here, and so does my long and laborious work of transcribing its contents as I have promised "that he should run, who readeth it."

Pensively turning over the written pages strewn on the table, I felt that I was full of ideas, emotions, and sensations accumulated during the long process of putting them on paper.

And I knew that, not only were the mysteries of the antediluvian world revealed to me, but a thread had been put into my hands to lead me through the maze of the postdiluvian world.

For the understanding of the contents of the roll I had resorted to the first two chapters of the book of Genesis. But now I would turn to all the rest of the Scripture, and all the inspired and ingenious works of our sages would be at my disposal for a comprehensive understanding of the past and the present of the postdiluvian world, in which we live now, and even of its future, the last days.

Thus I shall now begin with the third chapter of the book of Genesis, which speaks of Abraham, Isaac and Jacob—the first,

choicest vines planted in the vineyard of the Lord of hosts—
and I will continue to chronicle the life of the vineyard, as told
in the Scripture, in the elucidating and elating light of the
heavenly wisdom's works in the house of Israel. Works that
were direct, visible and miraculous, or indirect, invisible, but
inspirational, which took place on the long road to the realization of the heavenly wisdom's goal in man's world.

Moreover, from the following parts of this work we shall
learn not only of the heavenly wisdom working in the house of
Israel, but also of the fact that the (H)Ebrews possess two
innate qualities, aversion to bloodshed and an inclination to
meditativeness. Thus they were chosen to become the vineyard
of the Lord of hosts.

7

"For the vineyard of the Lord of hosts is the house of Israel, and the men of Judah a plant of his pleasures,"[1] and its first, choicest vine was Abraham, the son of Terah.

Abraham was planted in the vineyard because he was a (H)Ebrew, of the seed of Eber, and he was the first soul in the world who succeeded in breaking through the Satanic, obfuscating veil of paganism and forcing his way to the divine light of the true faith in the Lord God, Creator of the Universe.

Abraham was brought up in Ur of the Chaldees in his father's house, which was full of images and idols of the abominations. He was thus from his birth submerged in the pagan mire of his generations. Yet in the course of time he had striven against the idols and prevailed.

From his childhood Abraham was a keeper of his father's sheep, and in the long wakeful nights his eyes wandering in the skies would view the great display of celestial magnificence, with the result that Abraham gradually became aware of a new sensation. It seemed to him that the playfully winking stars

[1]Isa. 5, 7.

83

were trying to communicate to him something mysterious. Nay, it seemed to him that they were challenging him to try and find out what their twinkling lights were hinting at. But it all was too wonderful; so awesome he could not understand it.

Abraham's captivation by the fascinating vistas of the nightly skies did not interfere at all with his pagan way of life. Particularly so since, besides the moon, there were also some stars which the inhabitants of Ur of the Chaldees idolized.

Moreover, when clouds would block the sky or a thick fog would cover the face of the earth, fear would creep into Abraham's heart and he would remember the idols of Ur and of his father's house, calling on them for protection. And more than that; it came to pass that one night besides being enraptured with the majestic display of the starry skies, Abraham began to think of the skilled workers whose workshops were always full of ready-made idols.

Abraham admired their craftsmanship, by which they were capable of making any mask, any graven mask, any statue of an idol. Capable of making any idol...any idol whatever...any...

At this point, casting a glance at the idolized stars, Abraham felt as if he had been touched with a red-hot iron, for a heavenly spark of wisdom bounced from those stars and penetrated him inwardly.

The result was that a doubt entered his mind, a doubt which gradually deepened and consequently destroyed his devotion to the idols. For, as the divine spark turned into a flaming fire, it enlightened Abraham's mind, tearing him away from the obfuscating paganism and leading him instead into the lucid domain of spiritual abstract thinking.

The luster of the idols dimmed and their glory departed. In the morning Abraham would remain indifferent to the rays of the shining sun, in the light of which the celestial splendor would fade, and his eyes would see all around him the repulsive images of the idols which his fellowmen beseiged with incense and offerings.

Finally, Abraham's mind rejected the idols. His faith in the idols vanished altogether and he feared them no more. He openly spoke revolt against them, for in his eyes they were contemptible, worthless things.

Abraham would contentedly recall the day when, pacing around in his father's house and looking derisively at the multitude of idols that constituted Terah's sanctuary, he began to wreak havoc in his father's house, even trampling on the fragments of the broken pagan things that he had strewn all over the floor.

The influence of the divine spark of wisdom did not stop at this, but it began to awake and rejuvenate the heavenly potential of God's image and likeness, in which man was created.

The result was that a faint, subconscious conception of monotheism entered his enlightened and inspired mind. This conception led instantly to a question, a question without words, an awesome question without words and without an answer.

It was a frightening question. It was a question that caused great fear to take hold of him and fill his heart with anguish. And the question relentlessly and persistently stayed in his mind. Moreover, Abraham knew that the twinkling of the stars was challenging him to find an answer.

And so, on one such night, when Abraham's eyes were wandering in the starry skies and the hand of the pressing question was too hard upon him, it happened that the son of Terah, wearied to the utmost by his tormenting thoughts, jumped to his feet, stretched out his hands upward, and spontaneously burst into a desperate cry in which the pent-up question was finally heard aloud: WHO CREATED ALL THIS?

And behold, at that same moment a spark of the heavenly wisdom flared up in him with a sevenfold brightness, and Abraham's exalted soul reached the ingenious and divine conception of the Lord God, Creator of the heavens and the earth and all their hosts, "...and he believed in the Lord and he counted it to him for a righteousness."[2]

Thus it was Abraham the Hebrew who revealed to the world the true faith in the Lord God, Creator of the Universe. It may be presumed that his faith in God favorably impressed the members of his father's house, including Terah himself, inclining their hearts to follow Abraham and leave the pagan cult behind them.

It may also be presumed that Terah's conversion from idolatry might have provoked the fury of the inhabitants of Ur to oppose him and even to take vengeance on him and on his house.

So Terah took his household, except Nahar, and left with them for the land of Canaan. They came instead to Haran and dwelled there, and Terah died in Haran. But the land of Haran was also pagan, like Ur of the Chaldees. Therefore Abraham was inspired to leave that country and his father's house and go to dwell in the land of Canaan, which the Lord God promised to show to him.

Abraham was eighty-six years old when Hagar bore Ishmael to him. When Abraham was a hundred years old Sarah bore him a son, Isaac, "in whom Abraham's seed shall be called."[3] Ishmael dwelt in the wilderness of Paran, and his mother took him a wife out of the land of Egypt.

From the book of Genesis we know that Abraham made the oldest servant of his house, Eliezer by name, swear by the Lord, the God of heaven and the God of the earth, that he should not take a wife unto Isaac of the daughters of the Canaanites, but that he should go unto Abraham's country and to his kindred and take a wife from there.

Isaac was sixty years old when Rebekah bore him twins, Esau and Jacob. "And the boys grew, and Esau was a cunning

---

[2]Gen.I. 5, 6.
[3]Gen. 21, 12.

hunter, a man of the field. And Jacob was a plain man, dwelling in tents."[4]

Again do we know from the book of Genesis that Isaac called his son Jacob and blessed him and charged him and said unto him: "Thou shalt not take a wife of the daughters of Canaan. Arise, go to Padan-aram, to the house of Bethuel, thy mother's father, and take thee a wife from thence of the daughters of Laban, thy mother's brother."[5]

All this shows that the souls of the Patriarchs cleaved to their faith in the Lord God, Creator of the Universe.

More than two hundred years passed after Abraham came to dwell in the land of Canaan, and his grandson's house still numbered only seventy souls. True, there was also Esau, the son of Isaac and Rebekah, a genuine Hebrew like his brother Jacob but only by birth, for Esau loved strange women and his wives were the daughters of the Canaanites. They turned his heart away from the faith of his parents and to the idols.

Moreover, Esau gave up altogether the land of Canaan, as it is written: "Esau took his wives and his sons and his daughters and all the souls of his house, and his cattle and all his beasts and all his substance, which he had got in the land of Canaan— and went into the country from the face of his brother Jacob. For their riches were more than that they might dwell together, and the land, wherein they were strangers, could not bear them because of their cattle. Thus dwelt Esau in Mount Seir; Esau is Edom."[6] Which means that Esau is the father of the Edomites.

The result was that only Jacob and his household remained in the land of Canaan, but what was their position therein? They were a tiny minority in the land of Canaan; they were strangers among the indigenous inhabitants of the land, for the

---

[4]Gen. 25, 27.

[5]Gen. 28, 1, 2;

[6]Gen. 36, 6, 7, 8.

Hebrews' trade was cattle ever since Abraham had come to dwell there.

Their cattle, their flocks, and herds filled the land, roaming through its length and breadth, wandering from pasture to pasture and from well to well, and this would very often provoke quarrels between the Hebrews' shepherds and those of the Canaanites.

When famine would strike the land, the Hebrews with all their substance would go down to the pastures of Egypt, or of the land of the Philistines, where, as important nomads, they would meet the Pharaohs of Egypt and the kings of the land of the Philistines.

At the beginning the nomads would be welcomed by the rulers, but the welcome lasted only a short time. As can be seen, for instance, from what happened to Isaac, who was the only one of the Patriarchs that tried to occupy himself with farming in the land of the Philistines.

It is written: "Then Isaac sowed in that land and received in the same year a hundredfold; and the Lord blessed him. And the man waxed great and went forward and grew until he became very great, for he had possession of flocks and possession of herds and great store of husbandry, and Philistines envied him. And all the wells, which his father's servants digged in the days of Abraham his father, the Philistines had stopped them with earth. And Abimelech said unto Isaac: Go from us, for thou art much mightier than we. And Isaac departed thence and pitched his tent in the valley of Gerar and dwelt there."[7]

Such was the precarious situation of the Hebrews among all their neighbors inside and outside the land of Canaan, a situation which Jacob bitterly deplored once after the Shecem affair: "You have troubled me to make me odious unto the inhabitants of the land even unto the Canaanites and the Perizzites; and I being a few in number, they will gather them-

---

[7]Gen. 26, 12-17.

selves together against me and smite me, and I shall be destroyed, I and my house."[8]

But on the other hand, it should not be forgotten that it was Jacob who exceeded both his father and his grandfather in fruitfulness, for he begot twelve sons and a daughter, becoming thus the progenitor of the twelve Hebrew tribes. Jacob's sons were also fruitful, and soon Jacob's house counted seventy souls.

So it could be expected that the twelve tribes would multiply and be so fruitful as to replenish the land of Canaan, and consequently become a great and mighty nation that would reveal God's name among the far and near neighbors, and the house of Israel would dwell peacefully in the land of Canaan, in the Promised Land, forever and ever.

They went down into Egypt because of the famine that struck the land of Canaan, and also because Jacob most fervidly wished to see his lost son, Joseph, as it is written: "And Israel said: It is enough, Joseph my son is yet alive. I will go and see him before I die."[9]

Yet, even after the famine, Jacob preferred to dwell in Egypt, in the land of Goshen, twelve more years until he died. Moreover, the Hebrews continued to dwell in Egypt even after Joseph and his brothers died.

At this point a question may be asked. Why did Joseph's brothers return to Egypt after the burial of their father in the cave of the field of Machpelah, deserting thus the land of Canaan, the land of their father and of their forefathers Isaac and Abraham?

Moreover, there could be no doubt that Joseph would nourish them with bread in the land of Canaan as he had nourished the people of Egypt. Yet such questions should be driven away like smoke that is driven away by the wind when the events, the

---

[8]Gen. 34, 30.
[9]Gen. 45, 28.

facts, are considered and judged, not by their appearances, but by the enlightening works of the heavenly wisdom in the vineyard.

Behold, just as Abraham had been inspired to go out of his country and from his kindred and from his father's house unto the land of Canaan, so was Jacob inspired to go into Egypt and sojourn in the land of Goshen. And that same inspiration had put the prophetic words into Joseph's mouth when he said to his brothers: "And God sent me before you to preserve you a posterity in the earth, and to save your lives by a great deliverance."[10] Those were prophetic words, foretelling that the children of Israel would sojourn in Egypt, in the land of Goshen, from where at the appointed time a preserved, enormous Hebrew posterity would emerge, capable of inheriting the land of Canaan.

For had the seventy souls of Jacob's house returned to the land of Canaan after the famine, or after their father's death, or even after the death of Joseph and of his brothers—and counting them ten times seventy souls—all the same their position in the Promised Land would not change.

And the heavenly wisdom knew from the beginning that the seed of Eber "...shall be a stranger in a land that is not theirs, and shall serve them, and they shall afflict them four hundred years. And also that nation, whom they shall serve, will I judge, and afterward shall they come out with great substance."[11]

With great substance did they come out of Egypt, with great material substance and with great wealth, with jewels of silver and with jewels of gold and raiment, but the most important substance was the multitude of "...six hundred thousand on foot that were men, beside children,"[12] a huge camp of freed slaves which would be eventually molded into a nation by the son of Amram.

---

[10]Gen. 4, 5-7.

[11]Gen. 15, 13, 14.

[12]Ex. 12, 37.

Pondering now the Biblical era of the Hebrews, beginning with Abraham's coming into the land of Canaan and ending with his seed's exodus from Egypt, we may learn of the heavenly wisdom's glorious ways of caring for the vineyard of the Lord of hosts, for the house of Israel.

And we will learn of the heavenly wisdom's harmonious and inspirational works, most of them wrought quietly and naturally. Only when an impending disaster threatened the house of Israel with annihilation would the heavenly wisdom come to its rescue with miraculous, supernatural actions performed "with a mighty hand and with an outstretched arm and with great terribleness and with signs and wonders."[13]

Furthermore, we perceive also how the heavenly wisdom, which is the tool of His works, shaped a peculiar people in the land of Canaan.

When the Patriarchs became the first, choicest vines planted in the vineyard, the heavenly wisdom was pleased to see how the seed of Eber took root in the Promised land; how it brought forth buds, and how their divine, genuine, and shining faith in the one God, Creator of the Universe, was flowering in the dark pagan world, how the Patriarchs were fervently careful to maintain the purity of their faith. Seeing all this the heavenly wisdom knew that an eternal, threefold flower was shaped in the world, and that the seed of Eber—the house of Israel or the Hebrew people—was to be its stem forever and ever.

Shaping thus the threefold flower in the land of Canaan, the heavenly wisdom knew that the budding and the flowering of it were not enough for, while all this showed its spiritual essence, yet the material substance, or the earthly body of the flower was missing.

Therefore, the heavenly wisdom by indirect, inspirational works caused the Hebrews to go down to Egypt, where a multitude would be raised, becoming the bulk of the Hebrew nation, and all this in ways described in Genesis, as follows:

---

[13]Deut. 26, 8.

"And it shall come to pass, when Pharaoh shall call you, and shall say: What is your occupation? that you shall say: Thy servants' trade hath been about cattle from our youth even until now, both we and also our fathers; that you may dwell in the land of Goshen; for every shepherd is an abomination unto the Egyptians."[14]

Also: "And Pharaoh said unto his brethren: What is your occupation? And they said unto Pharaoh: Thy servants are shepherds, both we and our fathers. They said moreover unto Pharaoh: For to sojourn in the land are we come, for thy servants have no pasture for their flocks; for the famine is sore in the land of Canaan. Now therefore, we pray thee, let thy servants dwell in the land of Goshen. And Pharaoh spake unto Joseph, saying: Thy father and thy brethren are come unto thee, the land of Egypt is before thee; in the best of the land make thy father and brethren to dwell; in the land of Goshen let them dwell; and if thou knowest any men of activity among them, then make them rulers over my cattle."[15]

Should we not marvel again at the heavenly wisdom's glorious caring for the vineyard of the Lord of hosts? Behold, a handful of Hebrews were hurled into one of the great Empires of the ancient world. Seventy Hebrew souls were thrown into Egypt, an empire comparable to the Kingdoms of Assyria, Babylon and Persia.

Each of those empires was like a gigantic cauldron into which were thrown the remnants of those people that had been vanquished, decimated by the sword, enslaved and carried off from their native lands. Yet nothing of that kind could happen to the children of Israel in Egypt because, besides being isolated in the land of Goshen, a land of pastures, the Hebrews, as shepherds, were an abomination to the Egyptians and they could not be encroached upon.

---

[14]Gen. 46, 33, 34.
[15]Gen. 47, 3, 4, 5, 6.

And so Goshen was the most suitable land for cattle raising, and the Hebrews were welcomed to that nomadic paradise to raise enormous herds and flocks, which fact in its turn resulted in a very high fruitfulness for the house of Jacob so that, after four hundred years of dwelling in Goshen, six hundred thousand men on foot were ready for the Exodus.

And the son of Amram was assigned the task of molding into a nation the multitude of freed slaves, for the heavenly wisdom knew from the beginning that, as she had summoned the sons of God in the antediluvian world to cleanse the human flesh from the Satanic filth, in order to preserve a human posterity on the face of the earth, so would she summon the servants of God from the tribe of the Levites to save the lives of the children of Israel, not only from physical destruction, but also from the deep mire of paganism.

They will be summoned from the tribe of the Levites because in their midst ancestral traditions were remembered and kept. Also, a smouldering jealousy was alive in them for the Lord God of their forefathers Abraham, Isaac, and Jacob. And beside all this, they also harbored a jealousy for their inheritance, for the land of Canaan, the Promised Land.

Thus Moses would be summoned by the heavenly wisdom, and also his brother Aaron, who would be Moses' prophet. Moses would speak all that God commanded him and Aaron would speak to the Pharaoh.

And Moses, the servant of God and the greatest of all Prophets, would not only deliver the twelve Hebrew tribes from Egyptian bondage and bring them to the borders of the land of Canaan, but he would also instill in them the Lord God's Law, the Torah, by which they would live forever and ever, and by which the house of Israel would become a Kingdom of Priests and a holy nation.

8

It was Abraham who kindled a flaming light in the hills of Judea; an inextinguishable light of faith in the only Lord God, Creator of the Universe; a light that will glow forever and ever in the souls of his seed.

True, during the Egyptian bondage the glimmering light became barely visible, unable to penetrate the encompassing pagan darkness because the enslaved children of Israel served and kissed the Egyptian idol, the Egyptian calf.

Yet the divine spark of faith, which was smoldering in the depth of the Levites' hearts, would in the son of Amram, in Moses, flare up in a flaming fire of both faith in God and jealousy for his people, for the enslaved children of Israel.

Wandering with the flocks of Jethro from pasture to pasture in the open desert, Moses would leisurely ponder all the events that had taken place in Egypt before he fled from Pharaoh's palace. Soon his thoughts focussed on the horrible situation of his brethren, of his people, in Egypt.

At the same time his mind became flooded with reminiscences of the old traditions of the children of Israel; traditions that were kept up particularly by the Levites. Those traditions told him of the forefather Abraham, who abhorred idolatry and became the first believer in God; of the land of Canaan, promised to Abraham and to his seed after him; of the forefathers

Isaac and Jacob; of Joseph, the son of Jacob, who was once a ruler over Egypt; of the seventy souls that went down into Egypt. And all this ended with the enslavement of the children of Israel by the Egyptians, who made them serve with rigor.

Absorbed in such thoughts, Moses wandered with the flocks of sheep in the desert. Sometimes he would lead the flocks to the back of the desert. And once it came to pass that he came to the mountain of God, to Horeb, where an angel of the Lord appeared unto him in a flame of fire out of the midst of a bush, and where the Lord God spoke to him.

That vision threw him into an ecstasy of faith and confidence in the Lord God of Israel. An ecstasy which at once severed all his ties with Egypt. Standing at the foot of Mount Horeb, Moses felt that he was already cleansed from any trace of paganism, from any vestige of idolatry that might have adhered to him in Pharaoh's palace, where he was brought up by Pharaoh's daughter; where he spent his juvenile years till the day on which he slew an Egyptian evildoer.

Moses' mind plunged into feverish activity, and he knew that an end had come to his quiet and peaceful life in the house of his father-in-law. And also to his life as a shepherd who every morning would stand in awe of the majestic vistas that the rising sun would reveal to him, and particularly of the awesome sight of the mysterious Horeb.

Thus his idyllic pastoral life came to an abrupt end. After the vision of the burning bush Moses knew that the time had come for him to work. He was not an Egyptian any more.

He was now one of the children of Israel: one of the sons of the tribe of the Levites devoted with all his heart, with all his soul, and with all his might to the task of delivering his people from the Egyptian bondage, to the great task of molding a nation.

Moses returned to Egypt. He lived among his brethren, being able thus to watch closely and learn their way of life, their relationships, their traditions, their hopes and their frustrations—also their attitude towards their redemption from Egyptian bondage.

So Moses together with Aaron went to meet the elders of the children of Israel, and Aaron told them all the words which the Lord had spoken to Moses: that the Lord remembered them and that He had seen their affliction. Aaron encouraged them saying that their salvation was near. Seeing that the people believed, and that they bowed their heads and worshipped, Moses and Aaron went to Pharaoh and said to him: "Thus says the Lord God of Israel: Let my people go, that they may hold a feast unto me in the wilderness."[1] And the miraculous Exodus had begun.

Surely the deliverance of the house of Israel had begun, from the house of bondage in which they had spent four hundred years; in which the Hebrews as a nation had spent their youth and their juvenile years, and due to which they had become strongly attached to the Egyptians' way of life and to their deities—to serving and kissing the calf.

And Moses knew that he would have to perform two tasks: to bring them out of Egypt and also to bring them into the land of Canaan.

Moreover, the servant of God, the greatest of all Prophets, knew that he was assigned by the Lord God of Israel to restore the Hebrews to their deserved status in the world. To restore the divine threefold thread which had been shaped in the land of Canaan, in the days of the Patriarchs.

True, Moses knew that of the three essentials of which the divine thread was woven, he possessed only one: his faith in the Lord God of Israel. But Moses' all-embracing, penetrating, ingenious, and prophetic mind knew also that his faith was to become the active, inspiring, binding, and life-giving element which would effectuate the creation of the everlasting threefold bond, or cord, or knot consisting of the Promised Land, the

---

[1]Ex. 5, 1.

house of Israel and the Lord God of Israel, God of Abraham, Isaac, and Jacob.

Moses knew thus that the most important thing was to implant in their hearts faith in the Lord God of Israel; to instill love of God in the children of Israel; to make them aware that the Lord God only should they serve and to Him only should they cleave with all their hearts, with all their souls, and with all their might.

Moses did everything possible to achieve this. Three months after Pharaoh sent the Hebrews out from Egypt, "Moses brought forth the people out of the camp to meet with God, and they stood at the nether part of Mount Sinai,"[2] and descending from the top of the mount Moses proclaimed the ten commandments.

The impatient and unyielding prophet thought that his efforts would at once put an end to all the difficulties arising from the Hebrews' pagan defilement caused by the long Egyptian bondage.

But soon came the golden calf affair that caused Moses to break the tables of the Covenant, with the resulting horrible massacre of three thousand people by the sword of the Levites.

Afterwards some other deplorable events took place in the camp. From these Moses learned that his people were stiff-necked and rebellious, to which fact Moses reacted with increased and extended efforts to instill in them the knowledge of God and His law.

By God's command Moses went up unto Mount Sinai for the second time to hew two tables of stone, on which the ten commandments would be again engraved by God's finger, and which he would bring back into the camp to restore to the people their divine covenant made with the Lord God of Israel, who proclaimed the house of Israel to be His peculiar people.

On his way up the mount Moses noticed the fragments of the

---

[2]Ex. 19, 17.

broken tables of the covenant, and his heart was filled with grief. Suddenly a new thought flashed through his mind and he felt that he would not break the new tables, even if he saw his people dancing around the golden calf again. And this was followed by a startling question: will not the tables be lost anyhow in the flow of time?

Moses was confused, but for a short while only, for it dawned upon him that the two tables of testimony were presented to him as a symbol of God's wondrous works accomplished in the house of Jacob. Just as the ten commandments had been engraved on the tables of stone with the finger of God, so were they engraved on the hearts of the Hebrews. The ten commandments had been engraved on hearts of stone, but the time would come when the hearts of stone would become hearts of flesh in which a flaming faith in God would never be extinguished. Such were Moses' thoughts when he went up for the second time to Mount Sinai.

And the greatest of all prophets plunged into feverish activity in the role of a ruler, judge, lawmaker, architect, and strategist.

He had to write down into the Book all the commandments, ordinances, judgments, and statutes which the Lord God commanded him, and also to teach his people, particularly the Levites, how to keep and perform them.

Especially elaborated was the ritual code of offerings, of sacrifices. That ritual was initiated by Noah, and was renewed by the Patriarchs. It continued to live in the house of Jacob as an unforgettable tradition, as a sacred ritual of serving the Lord God of Israel.

It had been dormant in the Hebrews all the years of Egyptian bondage, and it had been awakened in them by Moses, who said to Pharaoh: "Let us go three days journey into the desert and sacrifice unto the Lord our God."[3] We knew also that Moses said to Pharaoh: "...our cattle also shall go with us;

---

[3]Ex. 5, 3.

there shall not an hoof be left behind, for thereof must we take to serve the Lord our God, and we know not with what we must serve the Lord until we come thither."[4]

And Moses eagerly hastened to fulfil God's commandment, which said: "...and let them make me a Sanctuary that I may dwell among them."[5] Zealously he embarked on the construction of the Tabernacle in the wilderness, a portable Sanctuary, the only holy place where they were to serve the Lord their God with sacrifices.

Moses knew that it would require a great effort to incline the hearts of his people unto their God. Surely this would be a powerful visual presentation before all the assembly of the congregation of the children of Israel.

And indeed a magnificent sight had been presented to them after the erection of the Tabernacle had been completed. The sight of Aaron, the High Priest, "in his beautiful garments with the ephod upon him and girded with the curious girdle of the ephod; also the breastplate upon him, and in the breastplate the Urim and Thumim; also the mitre upon his head and upon the mitre, even upon his forefront, the golden plate, the holy crown."[6] Also the sight of the other priests, Aaron's sons, who were clothed with coats and girded with girdles, with bonnets upon their heads. The sight of the Levites in clean washed clothes. And in particular the sight of the solemn services ministered by Aaron and his sons, with the Levites waiting upon them.

And Moses knew that all this turned into one grandiose, splendid sight which would awaken in his people a feeling of national pride, a feeling of self-confidence, and above all a feeling of confidence in the Lord their God whose strong arm would always protect and guard them.

Thus Moses had to occupy himself every day with various

---

[4]Ex. 10, 26.
[5]Ex. 25, 8.
[6]Ex. 29, 5, 6.

matters. While being engaged in the enormous architectural works of building the Tabernacle, he had to remain vigilant day and night in a state of self-defense against possible attacks by the many Nomadic tribes and other foes.

As a lawmaker and judge Moses had to consider and judge all the great matters and all the hard causes brought to him by the appointed "rulers of thousands, rulers of hundreds, rulers of fifties and rulers of tens."[7] As the ruler of the whole camp Moses had to listen to the people's claims, complaints, demands, and pretensions.

And if all that was not enough, there came to pass one day that a complaint against him was heard from his own flesh and blood, from his sister Miriam and brother Aaron, as it is written: "And they said: Hath the Lord indeed spoken only by Moses? Hath He not spoken also by us?"[8]

This happened in Hazeroth, where Miriam was removed from the camp seven days as a punishment for her complaint against Moses. Afterwards the people moved from Hazeroth and pitched in the wilderness of Paran, just at the southern border of the land of Canaan. And in that wilderness an unprecedented event occurred when the whole congregation revolted against Moses and proclaimed: "Let us make a captain and let us return into Egypt."[9] Their rebellious exclamation at the gates of the land of Canaan astonished the wilderness, and the Promised Land was ashamed to hear it from the seed of Abraham.

All this happened when, according to God's order, Moses sent the scouts to search the land of Canaan, an event that became a turning point on the road of the delivered Hebrews to the Promised Land.

When the scouts returned, bringing discouraging report of

---

[7]Ex. 18, 25.

[8]Num. 12, 2.

[9]Num. 14.

the land which they had searched, Moses watched the whole scene that passed before his eyes. A scene which is so dramatically described in the book of Numbers:

"And all the congregation lifted up their voices and cried; and the people wept that night. And all the children of Israel murmured against Moses and against Aaron. And the whole congregation said unto them: Would God that we died in the land of Egypt; or would God we had died in the wilderness; and wherefore hath the Lord brought us unto this land to fall by the sword that our wives and our children should be a prey? Were it not better for us to return unto Egypt? And they said one to another: Let us make a captain and let us return into Egypt. Then Moses and Aaron fell on their faces before all the assembly of the congregation."[10]

Oh that night, the mysterious stillness of the wilderness was disrupted, not by howling winds, nor by the howling of animals or beasts, but by the vociferous wailings of the whole congregation.

Moses felt that the lifted, wailing voices of the congregation had awakened him from a delightful reverie—as if he was brought down from a soaring flight, from a blissful hovering over the wilderness, over the camp, and even over much of the land of Canaan. And from this height he was brought down to feel that all his hidden and cherished aspirations had been shattered.

---

[10]Num. 14, 1-5.

9

A desolate Moses secluded himself in his tent, and it was now Moses the Prophet, the greatest Prophet "like unto whom there arose not a prophet since in Israel,"[1] who sunk into meditations on the events of the previous night. Moses remembered the scouts' evil report, which he wrote down into the Book and which he reiterated now to himself.

"We came unto the land whither thou sentest us, and surely it flows with milk and honey and this is the fruit of it. Nevertheless the people be strong that dwell in the land, and the cities are walled and very great; and moreover we saw the children of Anak there. We be not able to go up against the people, for they are stronger than we. The land through which we have gone to search is a land that eateth up the inhabitants thereof, and all the people that we saw in it are men of a great stature, and there we saw the giants, the sons of Anak, which come of the giants. And we were in our own sight as grasshoppers, and so we were in their sight."[2]

Thus Moses saw that, except for the few words "surely it flows with milk and honey and this is the fruit of it," all the rest of the report expressed a panicky fear of war, which fear the

---

[1] Dt. 34, 10.
[2] Num. 13. 27-33.

whole congregation took up instantly so that they broke out in wailing.

Moses knew that it could not have been otherwise since the scouts were the heads of the tribes. If then out of twelve of them ten brought an evil report, the whole assembly of the congregation would believe them, and would naturally become panicky and explode in the desperate outcry about returning into Egypt.

At this point Moses felt that the report of the searchers had not only awakened him from his reveries, but also caused him to search his own stance, his attitude toward the task assigned to him by the Lord God of Israel, and also his attitude towards his people with whom God made a covenant on Mount Sinai.

Moses perceived that from the very beginning, since the plagues had begun to come down on the Egyptians, he had lived in a world of superhuman actions, of divine signs, wonders, and miracles.

Behold, after the miraculous redemption of the people from the house of slavery came many miracles, of which the most outstanding were the miracles of the Manna, of the Quails, and of "the rock that turned into a standing water and the flint into a fountain of waters."[3] And Moses knew that all this resulted in the phenomenal fact that he was out of his human nature, living in a preternatural world.

As to his attitude toward his people, Moses remembered that, from the day "he went out unto his brethren and looked at their burdens."[4] he knew them as a multitude of slaves that lived a hopeless, totally submissive life, always remaining in constant fear lest they should provoke the anger of their masters.

Moreover, Moses knew that, of all their natural fears, the fear of war was the strongest in them. And this can be corroborated by the following passage from the book of Exodus: "And

---

[3]Ps. 11. 4, 8.
[4]Ex. 2. 11.

it came to pass when Pharaoh had let the people go, God led them not through the way of the land of the Philistines, although that was near, for God said, lest peradventure the people repent when they see war, and they return to Egypt."[5]

Thus Moses knew that his task was to lead the people, not through the land of the Philistines, but through the wilderness of Paran, just to the southern border of the land of Canaan. As a ready and ecstatic strategist, he would lead the twelve tribes through the mountains of the land where the Lord God's strong arm would smash the pagan kingdoms in pieces, as it had cast Pharaoh's chariots and his host into the sea, "...for the Lord is a man of war. The Lord is His name."[6]

And he, the ready ruler, would then cause the twelve tribes to inherit the Promised Land, while he, the ready architect, would erect a magnificent Sanctuary "that God may dwell among them." And he, the servant of God, would mold a nation to which God's Law had been bestowed on Mount Sinai. And thus will be accomplished the weaving of the threefold cord which had been outlined in the days of the Patriarchs in the land of Canaan.

Such were the thoughts of Moses' heart while moving closer to the borders of the Promised Land and camping in the wilderness of Paran.

Moses was elated and exalted. He was carried away by thinking of the forthcoming entry into the land promised to Abraham and his seed after him, and he was so full of exaltation that "the skin of his face shone."[7]

Yet in the wilderness of Paran all this had been thrown into confusion by the scouts' discouraging report, and Moses was brought back to earthly reality. He perceived that God's command to search the land had come to test the children of

[5]Ex. 13, 17.
[6]Ex. 15. 3.
[7]Ex. 34. 30.

Israel—to know whether their hearts, their souls, their spirits were closer to God and to His Law as their feet were closer to the gates of the land of Canaan. To reveal the people's stance, the people's attitude toward their redemption from bondage.

And it dawned on Moses that, while he was soaring high on wings of heavenly revelations, his people were sunk in uneasiness, discontent, and constant complaints. In the wilderness of Paran Moses' eyes opened to see that, while his aspirations were for a divine and blissful future in the Promised Land, his people's eyes were continually turned back to Egypt, the land of Goshen and to the Egyptian deity, the calf.

Moreover, after that weeping night Moses learned that his people were constantly homesick, for in their minds, in their eyes, Egypt remained their home, a home of plenty: of eating bread to the full, of the flesh pot and of fish.

In the wilderness of Paran for the first time Moses was astonished to realize that he just could not recognize his people. The vociferously crying, weeping, and wailing twelve tribes of the house of Jacob—were they his people, who had seen with their own eyes all the miracles, signs and wonders of the past few months?

Were they his people, the same people who together with him had sung on the seashore a wonderful song to the Lord? Were they his people who proclaimed at Mount Sinai, "...all that the Lord hath said will we do, and be obedient"?[8]

In the wilderness of Paran Moses saw before him a multitude totally estranged from the Lord God of Israel. A multitude that totally denied and repudiated the heavenly idea of their redemption from Egypt, the only purpose of which was to cause them to inherit the Promised Land wherein a kingdom of priests and a holy nation would be established.

Thus Moses heard God's words telling him that they should turn into the wilderness by way of the Red Sea to begin the

---

[8]Ex. 24, 7.

forty-years-long wandering between Egypt and Canaan; that it would be as a punishment for the sinful report of the scouts, who spent forty days searching the land; that during those forty years the generations would fall in the wilderness, and that only their children would inherit the land of Canaan under the guidance of Joshua, the son of Nun.

Yet at the same time Moses was seized with sad feelings. He felt as if he were guilty somehow of having neglected his people, who could not understand his exaltation and could not attain it.

Moses knew also that he would not go over the Jordan; but that Joshua would go over before his people and would cause them to inherit the Promised Land.

To dispel the sad thoughts Moses went out into the camp. It was the last day of their camping in the wilderness of Paran. He walked around avoiding the stigmatized adults. He watched the youth, the small children, the infants, whom, by God's grace, he would lead to the banks of the Jordan River.

Moses saw clearly the task assigned to him. He would have to raise the young generations, implanting in them faith and trust in the Lord God of Israel. The young generations that would never speak of the flesh pot and fish of Egypt. He thus knew that the young generations had become the sheep of his pasture and he their shepherd.

Surely, again he was a shepherd, as he was once in the land of Midian, where by divine inspiration he conceived the idea of weaving the threefold thread of the Holiness of the Lord God of Israel, His chosen people, and the land of Canaan.

But at this point the weeping, wailing night came to his mind, and instantly doubts were stirred up in him. He doubted whether, despite all his efforts, he would succeed in weaning his people from heathenism, because on that weeping night Moses perceived what kind of a patrimony the young generations would inherit from their fathers; what an awful pagan heredity would be transmitted to them. An horrible heredity of idolatry deeply rooted in their ancestors during four hundred years of rigorous slavery.

We know that, even after five hundred years had passed since Exodus, the diabolical, magnetic pagan power of the Egyptian calf was still so strong in the house of Jacob that Jeroboam succeeded in persuading ten Hebrew tribes to establish their pagan kingdom, as it is written: "Jeroboam made two calves of gold and said unto them: Behold thy gods, O Israel, which brought thee up out of the land of Egypt. And he set the one in Bethel and the other put he in Dan."[9]

Absorbed in his tormenting doubts Moses continued to walk around the camp, until the setting sun caused him to turn his eyes in the direction of the mount of God, Mount Horeb, as though taking leave of the heavenly visions he saw and of the divine sounds he heard thereon. The divine sounds of which it is written: "Moses spoke, and God answered him with a voice."[10]

As darkness fell Moses returned to his seclusion, sunk in the harassing doubts which were summed up in a worrisome and frightening question: If it is to be so, then what hope is there for Israel? And in answer to Moses' anxious question the Lord God of Israel put His good hand upon him."[11]

Full of knowledge, understanding and wisdom, Moses knew that a new task had been set before him, and his mind turned from the Exodus to the Hebrews' exodus from the land of Canaan. Moses knew that the deliverance of his people from Egypt had to be done in a miraculous way which could not be deferred because the truculent Pharaoh had resolutely intended to wipe out the remembrance of the house of Jacob from under the sun. The Pharaoh had charged the midwives that "...if it be

---

[9]I Kings 12. 28, 29.
[10]Ex. 19. 19.
[11]Esr. 8. 18.

a son, you shall kill him."[12] Later he charged all his people, saying: "Every son that is born—you shall cast into the river."[13]

Not so was the Hebrews' exodus from the land of Canaan. The seventy souls of the house of Jacob went down to Egypt because of no violent threat to their existence. They had to go there for the purpose of building up the material body of the Hebrew nation to raise in a natural way a multitude of six hundred thousand men, in addition to children.

Thus, when the greatest prophet found himself at the head of his redeemed people in the wilderness outside Egypt, he knew that his task would be to bring back into the land of Canaan the freed host to meet therein the destiny of God's peculiar people; to meet the holy destiny that hovered all those centuries over the land of Canaan, while waiting for the final stage of the threefold thread to be carried out.

Moreover, in his imagination Moses saw the spiritual destiny fluttering in the air before him. His people were scattered all over like leaves, and only Caleb and Joshua cleaved to their destiny. Joshua and Caleb, two valiant souls who openly denied the evil report saying: "Only rebel not ye against the Lord, neither fear ye the people of the land. The Lord is with us; fear them not; and all the congregation bade stone them with stones."[14]

But the greatest prophet knew that, as his people's success in achieving the national fulfillment had been accompanied while sinking in a pagan mire, so would the restoration of their national spiritual fullness and greatness be accompanied while sinking in a bloody mire.

Furthermore, Moses' prophetic eye perceived the natural process of their spiritual transmutation. Unlike the material restoration of their national tribe, which was achieved by forces coming from outside and even being forced on them,

---

[12]Ex. 1. 16.

[13]Ex. 1. 22.

[14]Num. 14. 9, 10.

their spiritual restoration would have to come from within, and would depend on the people themselves, even on every soul of them. It would depend on their own choice, according to the truthful saying that "all depends on God, except fear of God."

And Moses' prophetic eye saw that his burning aspirations to see his people delivering themselves from idolatry just after the Sinai revelations would be fulfilled, but only after a thousand years, when the sons of Judah and Benjamin would return to their border from the Babylonian captivity totally weaned from idolatry.

His prophetic eye saw also how a kingdom of priests would be established by them. A Hebrew kingdom in which everyone's heart would be whole with the Lord God of Israel, and in which the woven threefold thread would become a reality. Such were Moses' heavenly visions on the last night of camp in the wilderness of Paran. Great and elated visions of the far future of his people. At the same time Moses knew that those visions would materialize, based on accomplishments in the following forty years.

The greatest prophet knew that, by the grace of God, he, Moses, would accomplish the work of filling up the rolls of the book of the Law with God's statutes, ordinances, judgments, and commandments, while the body of his people, their twelve tribes, would steadily move closer to the Promised Land where the waiting spiritual destiny would be clothed with the contents of the Torah, to become eventually his people's tree of life, after their hearts of stone had turned into hearts of flesh. To be his people's tree of life, as a sign and a wonder in the sight of all the nations of the world.

Moses awoke from his prophetic visions, and at daybreak he was seen at the head of the camp going into the wilderness by the way of the Red Sea. He knew that it was the first day of the forty-year-long march to the Jordan River, and also the first day of his people's thousand-year-long road to find their God, with whom they just met at Mount Sinai.

To find the Lord God of their forefathers Abraham, Isaac,

and Jacob, to find Him and remain whole with Him forever and ever.

And as Moses, the servant of God, had once been seen lifting his rod and stretching out his hand over the sea to divide its waters, so was he seen on the day of his turning from the wilderness of Paran, lifting up the sword and stretching out his hand over the desert that lies between Egypt and the eastern borders of the land of Canaan.

As the years dragged on, the camp continued to wander in the desert, led by Moses the man, the meek man, of whom it is written: "The man Moses was very meek, above all the men which were upon the face of the earth."[15]

He was meek, for he never wanted anything for himself. All his life he was full of jealousy for the Lord God of Israel and for his people. His constant, burning desire was to see his people cleaving to God with all their hearts, with all their souls, and with all their might.

Seeing their stiff-necked ways and how they continued to be stubborn, impudent, and rebellious the same way their parents and grandparents were, Moses tried to instill in them fear of God.

Moreover, their attitude towards the Lord God's covenant and His commandments seemed to him to be monstrous, and he often exploded in a torrent of harsh words, curses, and abjurations. In vain were all his efforts to penetrate their closed ears, their obfuscated minds, or their uncircumcised hearts—to persuade them that they would never fully possess the Promised Land unless they were purged totally of idolatry.

A lengthy portion of such curses can be found in the book of Leviticus, but the most concentrated curses can be found in the book of Deuteronomy, in the twenty-eighth chapter. It consists of sixty-eight verses, and only fourteen of them contain blessings, while more than fifty contain curses, each curse more awful than the last.

---

[15]Num. 12. 3.

Moses was outraged that men be so foolish and unwise; to be so crooked and perverse "as to forget the Lord their Father, who had made them and established them; who led them in the waste, howling wilderness; who carried them as the eagle bears her young on her spread wings."[16] But all the worrisome and irritating experiences would fade when at nightfall he secluded himself in his tent and the greatest prophet, the servant of God, occupied himself delighted with his writings, with filling up the rolls of the book of the law with God's words spoken to him, for "the Lord spoke unto Moses face to face, as a man speaks unto his friend."[17]

From time to time Moses would go over the written rolls, being greatly delighted to read God's words speaking of holiness. Thus he happened once to read a whole chapter in which were given in great detail the structural peculiarities of the bodies of the unclean animals, fowls, and fishes. The chapter ended with the following passages: "For I am the Lord that brought you up out of the land of Egypt to be your God. You shall therefore be holy, for I am holy. This is the law of the beast and of the fowl and of every living creature that moves in the waters, and of every creature that creeps upon the earth. To make a difference between the unclean and the clean, and between the beast that may be eaten and the beast that may not be eaten."[18]

He also read the passage which said: "And ye shall be unto me a kingdom of priests and a holy nation. These are the words which thou shalt speak unto the children of Israel."[19] And Moses pondered: Does it mean to say that to be holy or not depends on what man eats?

But at this point Moses remembered the words which said:

---

[16]Deut. 32, 6, 10, 11.
[17]Ex. 33. 11.
[18]Lev. 11. 45, 46, 47.
[19]Ex. 19. 6.

"...man does not live by bread only, but by every word that proceeds out of the mouth of the Lord does man live."[20]

The greatest prophet became electrified by those heavenly words. His prophetic scope widened and deepened. He saw not only the future but also the past; the beginning of Noah's world, of the postdiluvian world, of the world of good and evil in which we live now. And Moses knew that the divine expression "by every word" included the commandment, the only one commandment, given to Noah and his sons, the one commandment upon which our world was founded; the one commandment that vouched for the sacredness, the holiness of man's life, the one commandment the keeping of which crowns the human being with God's holiness and vouches for the presence of God's image in him, as it is written: "...for in the image of God made He man."[21]

And the greatest prophet read further: "This day the Lord thy God had commanded thee to do these statutes and judgments; thou shalt therefore keep and do them with all thine heart and with all thy soul. Thou hast avouched the Lord this day to be thy God and to walk in His ways, and to keep His statutes and His commandments and to hearken unto His voice. And the Lord had avouched thee this day to be His peculiar people, as He promised thee, and that thou shouldest keep ALL commandments."[22]

From these passages Moses knew again that by keeping ALL the commandments, including His word of the holiness of man's life, the peculiar people would become a holy nation. And as Moses' prophetic eye had seen his people becoming a kingdom of priests after a thousand years had passed from the day of their deliverance from Egypt, so did his prophetic eye see his people becoming a holy nation after five hundred more

---

[20]Deut. 8. 3.
[21]Gen. 9. 6.
[22]Deut. 26. 16, 17, 18.

years had passed from the time the kingdom of priests had been established. A holy nation that totally repudiated bloodshed and the use of the sword.

Thus Moses was delighted to see his people's holy future, but what was their present in the wilderness? Moses knew that he would continue to instruct, to teach his people in two basic things: He would try to inure them to war, to bloodshed; and he would try to wean them from worshipping the calf and serving other idols.

But he knew that the seed of Eber was indestructible, for whenever total destruction threatened its existence, rescue would come in a miraculous way, as it had been delivered from Egypt. On its long road to find its Lord God and establish a kingdom of priests, its only spiritual food, sustaining it in the crucible of idolatry and bloody afflictions, would be the book of the law, the Torah.

And when Moses had ended writing the book of the law, he knew that the tables of the covenant of the Lord would be put inside the ark, which would be placed in the most holy part of the sanctuary, within the veil, to remain inaccessible therein to everybody except the High Priest. But as to the book of the law "Moses commanded the Levites, which bare the ark of the covenant of the Lord, saying: Take this book of the law, and put it in the side of the ark of the covenant of the Lord your God, that it may be there for a witness against thee."[23]

Thus Moses wished to make the book of the law accessible to the Calebs and Joshuas of the future generations; to make the book accessible to the men of spirit who will eagerly seek God's word and, finding it in the book "...will fill their bowels with it, and it will be in their mouths like honey for sweetness."[24]

The men of spirit, who all their lives would guard the book of the law, hiding it from their people lest pagan hands should destroy it.

---

[23]Deut. 31. 25, 26.
[24]Ez. 3. 3.

The men of spirit, the learned men, who will arise in the house of Jacob: the priests, the Levites, the scribes and above all the prophets—a breed of men of spirit whose task will be to fulfill the greatest prophet's prophecies and aspirations: to effect the weaving of the threefold thread in the Promised Land.

The prophets of the Lord God, a particular breed of the men of spirit, who will possess all the attributes necessary for the successful achievement of removing the pagan evil from the house of Israel.

Behold, "their faces will be made strong against the faces of their people, and their foreheads strong against the people's foreheads. As adamant and as hard as flint will be the prophets' foreheads, and they will not fear them, neither will they be dismayed at their looks, though they be a rebellious house."[25]

Those prophets will be indefatigable in their efforts "to cry aloud lifting up their voices like a trumpet to show God's people their transgression and the house of Jacob their sins."[26]

Beside the properties described, the prophets would also possess a divine spiritual attribute inherited from the greatest prophet, the father of all the prophets—understanding and wisdom which they would try to instill into the minds of their people.

The prophets' efforts would be aimed at convincing their people that "...God's word is very nigh unto thee, in thy mouth and in thy heart, that thou mayest do it."[27] It would thus tear them away from the background of obfuscation and fear, and set them on the ground of wisdom and understanding.

Wisdom and understanding, of which Moses prophesied: "Behold, I have taught you statutes and judgments, even as the Lord my God commanded me, that ye should do so in the land

[25]Ez. 3. 8, 9.
[26]Isa. 58. 1.
[27]Deut. 30. 14.

whither ye go to possess it. Keep therefore and do them, for this
is your wisdom and understanding in the sight of the nations,
which shall hear all these statutes and say: Surely this great
nation is a wise and understanding people."[28] And Isaiah, one
of the last great prophets, speaks of reasoning, saying: "Come
now, and let us reason together, says the Lord: though your
sins be as scarlet, they shall be as white as snow; though they be
red like crimson, they shall be as wool."[29]

Such were Moses' visions of the far future of his people.
They were camping in the land of Moab over against Jericho.
On the eastern banks of the Jordan were positioned the twelve
tribes of Israel, among them an army of a hundred thousand
warriors with swords.

Twelve tribes of Israel, each of them camped by its own
standard, and everyone of every tribe by the ensign of his
father's house. The twelve tribes brought with them to the
banks of Jordan the book of the law, the Torah, by the commandments of which they would live in the Promised Land.

At the head of the twelve tribes was Joshua, a mighty and
valiant man. True, he would not be able to drive out from
before him all the tribes of the land of Canaan and destroy their
kingdoms. Yet Joshua would succeed in establishing a strong
foothold, an indestructible foothold, in the land, and he would
cause all the pagan kingdoms to know his hand and his might,
for the Lord God of Israel was with him.

And in the land of Moab Moses heard God's commandment, saying: "Get thee up into this mountain Abarim, unto
Mount Nebo...and behold the land of Canaan, which I give
unto the children of Israel for a possession; and die in the
mount...and be gathered unto the people, as Aaron thy brother
died in Mount Hor and was gathered unto his people."[30]

---

[28]Deut. 4. 5, 6.
[29]Isa. 1, 18.
[30]Deut. 32. 49, 50.

This commandment had been spoken to Moses that selfsame day when he sung his last song in the ears of all the congregation of Israel.

Accordingly, "Moses went up unto the mountain of Nebo ...that is over against Jericho. And the Lord showed him all the land of Gilead unto Dan. And all Naphtali and the land of Ephraim and Menasseh and all the land of Judah, unto the utmost."[31]

But from the top of Mount Nebo Moses saw something more: He looked northeast—and he beheld Abraham the Hebrew leaving his country and his kindred and his father's house and bringing into the land of Canaan the true faith in the Lord God, Creator of the Universe; the true faith which he attained in Ur of the Chaldees.

Moses looked southwest. From there he, Moses, had just brought to the threshold of the land of Canaan the book of God's law, the Torah, which he received on Mount Sinai in the wilderness.

And in the most dazzling last flash of his ingenious mind Moses realized that from the very beginning the holiness of the Lord God had been concentrated on both His peculiar people and on the land of Canaan, on the shaping of the divine, indestructible threefold thread (knot) which was to become the source of the knowledge of God and His law—a divine vision which, as we know, had been prophesied by Isaiah: "...for out of Zion shall go forth the law, and the word of the Lord from Jerusalem."[32]

---

[31] Deut. 34. 1, 2.
[32] Isa. 2, 3.

10

"Israel served the Lord all the days of Joshua and all the days of the elders that prolonged their days after Joshua, and which had known all the works of the Lord that He had done for Israel. But after all that generation were gathered unto their fathers, there arose another generation, which knew not the Lord nor yet the works which He had done for Israel. And they did evil in the sight of the Lord, and served Baalim.... And the anger of the Lord was hot against Israel, and He delivered them into the hands of spoilers that spoiled them, and He sold them into the hands of their enemies round about, so that they could not any longer stand before their enemies. Nevertheless the Lord raised up judges, which saved them out of the hands of those that spoiled them.... And when the Lord raised them up judges, then the Lord was with the judge, and delivered them out of the hand of their enemies all the days of the judge. And it came to pass when the judge was dead that they returned and corrupted themselves more than their fathers, in following other gods to serve them, and to bow down unto them; they ceased not from their own doings, nor from their stubborn way."[1]

These passages reveal the pattern of the Hebrews' life in the Promised Land during a period of about a thousand years, from Israel's deliverance from the Egyptian bondage to the

---

[1]Jud. 2. 7-19.

deliverance of the sons of Judah and Benjamin from the Babylonian bondage.

The result was that in the inherited land of Canaan were left-over enclaves of pagan tribes, and soon the situation of the house of Israel seemed to be in a precarious condition. The seed of Eber seemed to be exposed to extinction either by the sword of its many enemies or by a gradual process of disintegration and dissolution among the multitudes of the indigenous inhabitants of the land of Canaan.

The house of Israel was rescued from the critical situation by Samuel, the prophet of the Lord and authoritative ruler over Israel. Samuel ushered in a new era, in which a turning point took place in the lives of the children of Israel.

Samuel as a child was brought into Shiloh to Eli, the priest of the tabernacle. He was brought there by his mother after she weaned him. She said to Eli the priest: "For this child I prayed, and the Lord has given me my petition which I asked of Him. Therefore also I returned him, whom I have attained by peti-tion, to the Lord. As long as he lives—he shall be lent to the Lord."[2]

Also: "And Samuel grew, and the Lord was with him, and did let none of his words fall to the ground. And all Israel from Dan even to Beersheba knew that Samuel was established to be a prophet of the Lord."[3]

Thus Moses' divine prophecy seemed to be fulfilled. The prophecy says: "The Lord thy God will raise up unto thee a prophet from the midst of thee, of thy brethren, like unto me; unto him you shall hearken." And behold, there was Samuel, the son of an ordinary man of Ramathaim-Zophim, of Mount Ephraim, whose name was Elkanah.

Samuel, who ministered unto the Lord in Shiloh from his youth, became consequently the recognized ruler over all

---

[2] I Sam. 1. 27, 28.
[3] I Sam. 3. 19, 20.

Israel, saving them from the hand of the Philistines in a wondrous, inspirational way so that they came no more into the borders of Israel all the days of Samuel.

Great was Samuel's spiritual influence on his people, and they put away the strange gods and Ashtaroth from among them. Yet their hearts did not become whole with the Lord their God, for they remained stony and unheeding of God's words of the book of the law, as the hearts of their fathers had been all the years of the era of the judges.

The difference between Samuel and the preceding judges was that, while the judges appeared unexpectedly to rescue Israel from a catastrophic situation, Samuel was known to the people from his childhood as a prophet of the Lord; a prophet crowned with a halo of godliness, and his people naturally recognized him as a ruler over them, particularly so in their trouble and affliction coming from the ruthless Philistines.

Samuel succeeded in establishing in Israel both his status as a prophet and that of an authoritative ruler for all the days of his life, as it is written: "And he went from year to year, and he circuited to Bethel and Gilgal and Mizpeh, and judged Israel in all those places. And his return was to Ramah, for there was his house, and there he judged Israel; there he built an altar unto the Lord."[4]

Thus it can be said that under the rule and guidance of Samuel the prophet, judge, ruler, and priest, an end had been put to the state of anarchy of the era of the judges, of which it is written: "Every man did that which was right in his own eyes."[5]

In his old age Samuel was ready to establish his dynasty, and he appointed his sons, who were judges in Beersheba, to be judges over all Israel. But his sons turned aside from their father's way, corrupting themselves by taking bribes and perverting judgment.

---

[4]I Sam. 7. 15, 16, 17.
[5]Jud. 21. 25.

Soon the elders of Israel came to Samuel at Ramah. They said to him: "Behold, thou art old, and thy sons walk not in thy ways; now make us a king to judge us."[6] Their demand was evil in his eyes and it angered him, but soon an inspired Samuel hearkened to their voices and fulfilled their urgent demand by giving them a king.

Thus Saul became the anointed king over Israel; a king who seemed to satisfy both Samuel and the people of Israel.

Judging by Saul's countenance and by the height of his stature—he was taller than any of his people—the people were confident that their king was a mighty and valiant man who would go out before them to fight their battles.

Moreover, when they learned that Saul was a Benjamite and that his family was the least of the tribe; when they knew that besides this Saul was a meek man—for he had hid himself when he was approached to be king—when they learned all this, they were sure that Saul would never be the kind of king Samuel was afraid of.

They remembered how Samuel had presented to them an awful image of the king that would rule over them: "He will take your sons and appoint them for himself...and some shall run before his chariots.... And he will appoint him captains over thousands and over fifties, and will set them to plow his ground and to reap his harvest.... He will take your daughters to be perfumers, and to be cooks and bakers. And he will take your fields and your vineyards and your olive yards, and give them to his servants. And he will take the tenth of your seed and of your vineyards and give to his officers and to his servants. And he will take your menservants and your maidservants and your goodliest young men and your asses and put them to his work. He will take the tenth of your sheep, and you shall be his servants."[7] But the people refused to listen to the

[6]I Sam. 8. 5.
[7]I Sam. 8. 11-17.

voice of Samuel, and thus they were given an anointed king to rule over them.

As to Samuel, he thought that the meek Saul would be clay in his hands. He, Samuel, would instruct him and guide him in the paths of God's law. He, Samuel, would strive to inculcate in Saul all the commandments, statutes, ordinances, and judgments of the book of the law. Moreover, Samuel introduced Saul to the circle of the prophets, as it is written: "...after that thou shalt come to the hill of God, where is the garrison of the Philistines, and it shall come to pass when thou art come thither to the city, that thou shalt meet a company of prophets, coming from the high place with a psaltery and a tabret and a pipe and a harp before them and shall prophesy. And the spirit of the Lord will come upon thee and thou shalt prophesy with them, and shalt be turned into another man."[8]

Samuel apparently strove to turn the plain and meek Saul into a king-prophet who would judge Israel by the statutes of God's law—as he, Samuel, had done all his life. Furthermore, Samuel's aspirations also included raising as many prophets as possible in the house of Israel.

The behavior of Samuel's prophets indicated that they developed to some extent a quality of self-denial, as can be seen from the following: "...and Saul stripped off his clothes also and prophesied before Samuel in like manner, and lay down naked all that day and all that night. Therefore they said: Is Saul also among the prophets?"[9]

Samuel's efforts to turn Saul into king-prophet—as he, Samuel had been a ruler-prophet—did not and could not come true because Samuel was above all a prophet of the Lord, and by his prophetic spirit ruled over Israel. The meek Saul, on the other hand, turned presumptive, as if he had been anointed, not with oil, but with self-conceit.

---

[8] I Sam. 10. 5, 6.
[9] I Sam. 19. 24.

When Saul joined the prophets' companies and began prophesying in their manner, he presumed to be Samuel's equal. And Saul began to build altars and to officiate as a priest, not only at peace offerings, but even at whole burnt offerings.

All this greatly angered Samuel, who said to Saul: "Thou hast done foolishly; thou hast not kept the statement of the Lord thy God."[10] And again Samuel rebuked Saul, saying to him: "...and the Lord sent thee on a journey and said: 'Go and utterly destroy the sinners, the Amalekites, and fight against them until they be consumed.' Wherefore then didst thou not obey the voice of the Lord, but didst fly upon the spoil, and didst evil in the sight of the Lord?"[11]

The dissension between them deepened and: "...Samuel went to Ramah, and Saul went up to his house, to Gibeah of Saul. And Samuel came no more to see Saul until the day of his death, though Samuel mourned for Saul."[12]

Thus Samuel grieved for his aspirations, which had been ruined as the life of Saul was ruined—a life of a wretch, obsessed by an evil spirit, instead of a life of a king-prophet molded by the prophet of the Lord.

And though Samuel came no more to see him, Saul, on the contrary, always sought to see the unforgettable "seer," the prophet who once raised him up from the dust, from the least family of Benjamin to be a king over Israel.

As to Samuel, we know that before he died he had one last task to perform assigned to him by the heavenly wisdom, to anoint Jesse's youngest son to be king over Israel.

Samuel's actions were directed and guided step by step by the Lord God of Israel. Samuel was led thus into Bethlehem, into the house of Jesse. When he saw Eliab, Jesse's oldest son, the prophet was greatly impressed by the look of his counte-

---

[10]I Sam. 13. 13.
[11]I Sam. 15. 18, 19.
[12]I Sam. 15. 34, 35.

nance and by the height of his stature, as he had been impressed once by the appearance of Saul. But the inspired prophet knew that the Lord God rejected him, "for the Lord looks on the heart, and not on the outward appearance."[13]

Jesse made his seven sons pass by, and Samuel knew again that God rejected them. Jesse then sent to the field for the youngest son, and when the ruddy, fresh-faced David was brought in, Samuel heard a small, still voice saying: "Arise, anoint him, for this is he."[14] Thus King David was found for the house of Israel.

Casting a look at the past era of the Judges, we perceive that the precarious situation of the house of Israel, and particularly their spiritual vacillations, reminds us somewhat of the wanderings of their ancestors in the wilderness between Egypt and the eastern banks of Jordan.

But then Moses was with them, his ingenious mind hovering over the camp day and night. While in the era of the judges the book of the law had to be kept in hidden places, and only its spirit remained hovering above, waiting for the fullfilment of Moses' double prophecy, and for the establishment of the kingdom of priests.

A kingdom where everyone's heart would be whole with the Lord God of Israel, and where the Promised Land would be wholly inherited and possessed by the house of Israel.

To Samuel was assigned the task of causing his people, all the twelve tribes, to set out on a road, a very long road, at the end of which that goal would be achieved.

All this means to say that before entering such a kingdom the Hebrews would have to purge themselves of any trace of heathenism—by passing through a severe trial, through a purgative crucible of afflictions and bloodshed.

Now, the word "kingdom" implies the rule of kings, which

---

[13] I Sam. 16. 7.
[14] I Sam. 16. 12.

means that the twelve tribes of Israel were to be led by kings, and not by prophets, a thing which Samuel learned from his experience with Saul. The use of the sword was totally inappropriate to the prophets.

Thus Samuel anointed two kings, and the twelve tribes plunged, at the very beginning of their fateful march to their destiny, headlong into a horrible internecine war between those kings.

At this point we should again marvel how wondrous are the heavenly wisdom's works in the vineyard of the Lord of hosts. The two kings were sons of two different tribes. Saul a son of Benjamin and David of Judah. And behold, at the end of the road, after five hundred years had passed since David's reign, of all the multitudes of the twelve tribes, only the remnants of Benjamin and Judah returned to their borders, while the other ten tribes were lost in the Assyrian crucible.

The sons of the two tribes had been encouraged by the inspired Cyrus, King of Persia, to return into Jerusalem under the ruler of Ezra and Nehemiah, who laid the cornerstone of the oncoming Maccabean kingdom of priests.

11

It should be said that as Samuel from his childhood ministered to the Lord in the Tabernacle of Shiloh, so did David from his youth minister to the Lord in the palace of nature with songs and with a harp. In the green hills of Bethlehem did he sing praises unto God, extolling Him and rejoicing before the Lord God of Israel.

In his infancy David was steeped in the spirit of the heritage of the house of Jacob; dipped in the spirit of the divine precepts of the book of the law and of the holiness of the ark of the covenant.

King David was crowned, not only with a royal crown, but also with the crown of poetry. His poetic psalms flutter on wings of a boundless and profound faith in God.

His psalms have since become a source of inspiration to men of spirit, for in exalted words they can pour out their hearts in time of distress before the Almighty, and also draw from the psalms consolation and courage which will enable them to continue walking in the way of righteousness, "...in the way which God knows."[1]

What was David's heart's desire? "To dwell all the days of his

[1]Ps. 1. 5.

life in God's house, there to behold the delight of the Lord and to visit in His temple."[2] But instead of all this, David's life was like a cauldron; a life full of wars and revolts; a turbulent life of conspiracies and of intrigues.

True, his heart was overflowing with godly intentions, but at the same time his passions were deep as the abyss, and the depth of the abyss amazed, shocked, and terrified David.

His nightmare began when once with wide-open eyes he dreamed of the unforgettable spectacle of his victory over Goliath, who dared to draw a sword against Israel in the valley of Elah. And then all of a sudden, instead of the taunting and haughty Philistine, Uriah the Hittite, mute and meek, appeared before his eyes.

David's countenance became an expression of sheer horror which caused his fingers to grip convulsively the object he held in his hands. And lo, this time it was not a sword, but the gittith, which almost broke in the strong grasp of his hinds. The delicate gittith emitted a faint groan, which drew David's attention to it.

At the sight of his favored instrument, his heart brightened with joy. The horrible vision vanished, and a sweet smile appeared on his lips, for he was again overtaken by a burning desire.

Did he not intend, when he picked up the gittith, to sing his affections for the woman he loved? Did he not intend to crown her with a most wonderful love song?

Oh Bathsheba...Bathsheba... But was she not the wife of a man? And all of a sudden David's face grew dark. As in a flash he perceived the meaning of the appearance of the Hittite before his eyes. It had come to remind him of his two victories. The victory over the mighty Goliath and also his victory over Uriah. Did not David watch the departure of the doomed Uriah to the walls of Rabbah, where he would be killed by the

---

[2]Ps. 27. 4.

sword? Did he not see how his faithful and brave warrior was filled with shame, because from the first day of Uriah's arrival into the king's palace he became subject of derision of the town's people? And was it not David who caused all that shame to come on the Hittite's head? On the head of Uriah, Bathsheba's husband?

In silence Uriah left, calm and collected, carrying in his pocket David's secret and despicable letter, but in his heart remaining a noble man of unreproachable honor and dignity who steadily refused to go down to his house, to his disgraced wife.

It was David who consumed like a moth Uriah's most cherished thing. And David had the feeling of being a moth when he met Uriah's last reproachful and scornful glance, which was his only answer to David's vileness and to the utterances of David's deceitful mouth.

That glance drove David into a frenzy, which raged in him for a few days until Joab's messenger brought the news that "...thy servant Uriah the Hittite is also dead."[3] And David's wrath subsided.

Yet a feeling unknown to him till then began to penetrate his heart; a feeling of contrition for what he had done to the Hittite. David was in low spirits. Even his still-burning desire for Bathsheba could not keep him from sullen groaning.

All day long he went on moaning. He was bent down under a heavy burden. Thus it took Uriah's piercing and reproachful glance a long time to convey to David's heart a sense of guilt, which made his life bitter, full of groans and moans of a shame and contrition that crumbled his confidence in his absolute righteousness.

David, who would always complain of wrongdoers all around him, found himself an evildoer who perpetrated the greatest evil against Uriah, toward whom he would not extend

---

[3] II Sam. 11. 24.

any mercy. Yet, while he was sinking in the depth of sin, a ray of hope suddenly flashed before his eyes.

Behold, something totally forgotten emerged from his memory, and the thought of his guilt dwindled and his spirits rose. His anguish vanished. No more would he grope in the dark, for he knew what to do. He would act according to the precepts of the book of the law, from which Zadoc had read to him a chapter concerning offerings brought to the altar.

It said: "When a ruler has sinned and done something through ignorance against any of the commandments of the Lord his God concerning things which should not be done— and is guilty, or if his sins wherein he has sinned come to his knowledge, he shall bring not a peace offering, but a sin offering of a goat, a male without a blemish."[4]

David's energy turned to the offerings. The fires on the altars were kept burning day and night because, besides the burnt and sin offerings, thousands of lambs, bullocks, goats, and rams were sacrificed as peace offerings in the name of King David.

The people that gathered around the altars were pleasantly surprised by the enormous number of sacrifices, and at the same time joyfully feasted on every good piece of meat the offerings so abundantly brought to the altars.

From the roof of his palace David watched the crowds that were noisily feasting, expressing joy and praises to their king. And David's lips whispered: "O Lord, before I was afflicted I did err."[5] And: "O Lord, rebuke me not in thine anger, nor chasten me in thy wrath."[6]

David seemed to be content with the bustle of the sacrifices, but inwardly he was longing for one thing only: to convince himself that he had commited the sin, not presumptuously, but due to his ignorance or by error. And finally David became

---

[4]Lev. 4. 22, 23.
[5]Ps. 9. 67.
[6]Ps. 38. 1.

firm in his belief that he was led astray by his foolishness and by his proclivity to indulge in the easy vices of the flesh.

But David was mistaken. The feeling of innocence never came back to his heart. On the contrary, the feeling of sin, of guilt, became stronger every day, and he was pressed under it, "as a cart is pressed that is full of sheaves."[7] The ghosts frequented him again, multitudes of them. They terrorized him, and in his ears thundered a voice: "Oh thou man, come out, come out thou man of blood."[8]

In the sincerity of his heart David thought that evil did not dwell within him. Did he not enact God's law and bring justice all around him? Did he not glorify God in numerous hymns?

David remembered how in the perilous moments of his life the Lord would answer his prayers, and he then would praise God before a large congregation, proclaiming: "He delivers me, because He delights in me."[8]

In vain did David look for a deliverance from his distress; in vain did he look for an encouraging thought, feeling, or a cheering word. His heart was fluttering, and his strength was failing him. He knew that a severe punishment had come down upon him to turn him into a wretch.

Moreover, he felt that the abomination of the evil he had done to Uriah was going to touch the apple of his eye. Touch his gift of being able to praise the Lord God of Israel, to whom he cleaved with all his heart.

Thus the son of Jesse, with his contrite and broken heart sunk to the depths of despair. Never before had he endured such an agony. He bemoaned his fate of being doomed to join those that would pine away in their iniquities.

And yet behold, generation unto generation would cry aloud ascribing greatness to the son of Jesse, for there was strength in him to bring forth from the innermost recesses of his heart into

---

[7]II Sam. 16. 7.
[8]Ps. 18, 19.

man's world a divine gift, the name of which is CON-SCIENCE, with its stings of remorse, penitence, and compunc-tion that can break man's heart.

And David, the bearer of two crowns, knew how to express his remorse openly and in a clear voice. The people were puzzled hearing their king and ruler expostulating with himself and lamenting that he was full of iniquities, and bemoaning his fate.

He was heard lamenting: "For I am ready to halt and my sorrow is continually before me. For I will declare mine iniq-uity and I will be sorry for my sin."[9] David knew that his spirit had been neither strong enough nor clean enough to be able to rule over evil, and in this lies the greatness of his soul.

For the son of Jesse had thus unknowingly established a new altar; an altar made neither of wood nor of stone, an altar that would rest in man's heart. An altar on which thenceforth the men of spirit would offer their hearts iniquities, an altar that would never be ruined by evil and on which the fires of the offerings would never die down.

David knew that his iniquities covered his head, and if from time to time his spirit rose to a heavenly height, after a while he fell back into the depths of sin.

David thus learned that man cannot withstand temptation, and therefore he put all his hope in penitence and forgiveness: "...with Thee is forgiveness, that Thou mayest be feared."[10]

Behold, even men of spirit, whose hearts are whole with God and who serve Him faithfully, even they live in constant fear lest they should stumble and fall into evil's net.

And no wonder, for we know that Evil succeeds very often in turning sincere repentance into "a precept of men, learned by rote."[11]

Now, David's greatness lies not only in the spiritual realm,

---

[9]Ps. 38. 17, 18.
[10]Ps. 130. 4.
[11]Isa. 29. 13.

but also in the material world. He smote all the enemies round about Israel, and united the twelve tribes of Israel into one nation, into a kingdom, over which he ruled forty years.

Moreover, David made Jerusalem the capital of his kingdom, and Jerusalem included the holy hill of Zion, which consequently became a hallowed site of the world, as it is written: "...out of Zion, the perfection of beauty, God has shined."[12] Also: "...blessed be the Lord out of Zion, which dwelleth at Jerusalem."[13]

Thus it should be said that the son of Jesse completed the [material] part of the task initiated by the greatest prophet, for he caused the twelve tribes to inherit all the land promised to Abraham, Isaac, and Jacob.

David made many wars against the numerous pagan tribes that had multiplied and waxed stronger and mightier in every corner of the Promised Land.

They incessantly harassed the twelve tribes of Israel with intrusive provocations and wars, and all this in addition to the continuous and ominous onslaughts of the insidious Philistines.

It was the son of Jesse who put an end to the precarious situation of the Hebrews in the land of Canaan, for he cut off not only the inhabitants of the pagan enclaves, but also the many and mighty outside enemies.

David succeeded in subduing the Philistines, the most ruthless and formidable enemy of the Hebrews.

Behold, it is written: "Now there was no smith found through all the land of Israel, for the Philistines said, lest the Hebrews make them swords and spears. But all the Israelites went down to the Philistines to sharpen every man his share and his coulter, and his ax and his mattock. Yet they had a file for the mattocks and for the coulters and for the axes and for the forks and to sharpen the goads."[14]

---

[12]Ps. 50. 2.
[13]Ps. 135. 21.
[14]I Sam. 14. 19-21.

The Philistines even placed garrisons in many cities of the Hebrews. The Philistines waxed stronger and more powerful, while the Hebrews became weaker and more defenseless.

Moreover, it seemed that something of a national disintegration began to take place among the sons of Jacob, and some of them openly joined the Philistines' camp. They despised Saul, saying: "How shall this man save us?" David also subdued the Edomites, and "...he put garrisons in Edom. Throughout all Edom put he garrisons and all they of Edom became David's servants."[15]

David's greatness struck the imagination of the people of Israel, filling them with such unforgettable wonder and awe that in every generation to this day they can be heard chanting on every suitable occasion the refrain "David king of Israel exists and is alive."

Certainly man's imagination could be affected overwhelmingly by David's stormy life, by his enormous successes and achievements, by his material and spiritual greatness.

His gigantic image overshadowed all his predecessors, all the judges that had ruled occasionally over Israel since Joshua. Yet, delving into the events that took place in the turbulent and entangled era of Samuel, Saul, and David, we shall come to the conclusion that "...because of King David, Israel exists and is alive."

David's cleaving to God was almost tangible in his ecstatic and exalted psalms, in which he extolled the Lord God of Israel, and in which he poured out incessantly his longings for nearness to God.

But lo, his susceptibility to the knowledge of evil was likewise so powerful that it plunged him into the most heinous and tragic affair with a man's wife, with Bathsheba, the wife of Uriah the Hittite.

How outrageous the evil was can be learned from Absalom's

---

[15]II Sam. 8. 14.

odious conduct, in which his father's sin echoed most shamefully, as it is written: "...so they spread Absalom a tent upon the top of the house and Absalom went in unto his father's concubines in the sight of all Israel."[16]

And the heavenly wisdom knew that as "...out of the strong came forth sweetness,"[17] so, out of the impact of the collision of the two contrary forces in David's heart would come forth into the pagan, somber world the divine gift of *CONSCIENCE*.

It would come to serve as a means of rousing in man's mind the concept of a self-inflicted purging recompense, a concept that became a reality in a world where man is his own judge and recompenser.

It came first on an individual level, and it broke David's spirit, and caused his heart to be broken and contrite. It is apt to cause man's mind to look back at the evil perpetrated by him with a feeling of horror, shame, disdain, and disgust.

David's triumphant outcry was that "...thou desirest not sacrifices that I should give it; thou delightest not in burnt offering. The sacrifices of God are a broken spirit; a broken and contrite heart, O God, thou wilt not despise."[18] When this outcry was heard, the heavenly wisdom knew that it would result in a momentous turning point in Israel's life.

For the sounds of David's outcry continued to reverberate in the house of Israel, in the vineyard of the Lord of hosts, in which the plants of God's delight, the men of spirit, the elated prophets were profoundly impressed and affected by the greatness of man's spirit and by its divine achievements in the world of good and evil.

And as they looked at the people, at their own people, at the offspring of Abraham, Isaac, and Jacob—and as they saw them wallowing in the deep pagan mire—the prophets of God

---

[16]II Sam. 16. 22.

[17]Jud. 14. 14.

[18]Ps. 51. 16, 17.

were overcome with a feeling of shame, scorn, and a sickening dislike, and above all with great anger.

In a flash the prophets conceived that their task in the vineyard was to be their people's conscience, which would never loose its hold over the people's spirit and hearts—not until heathenism had been put away in the house of Israel, in the vineyard of the Lord of hosts.

Thus the son of Jesse drastically changed the prophets' stagnant attitude towards their people into an offensive one. Surely King David unintentionally turned the self-complacent, self-satisfied, and introverted men of spirit into extroverted prophets; into valiant fighters against the plague of idolatry in Israel, in the vineyard of the Lord of hosts.

Their tenacious courage will result in their full success, in bringing about the greatest prophet's words that Israel was to become a kingdom of priests.

12

Nathan the Prophet was David's closest adviser in matters concerning the observance of the commandments, statutes, ordinances, and judgments of the book of the law, but soon the harmony between them was disturbed.

It all started on a day when the king and the prophet had a friendly conversation in David's palace, as it is written: "...the king said unto Nathan the Prophet: See now, I dwell in a house of cedar, but the ark of God dwelleth within curtains. And Nathan said to the king: Go, do all that is in thine heart, for the Lord is with thee."[1]

And David had made ready for the building, but soon Nathan brought God's word to the king, saying: "Thou shalt not build a house for my name, because thou hast been a man of war, and hast shed blood."[2]

These words of God had brought a new intimation to the prophets, and their ears received an inkling of a new concept that captivated their minds, for the suggestion was that the son of Jesse, whose hands were bloody, was unworthy to build a house in God's name because it would be inconsistent with the holiness and glory of the Lord God of Israel.

---

[1] II Sam. 7. 2, 3.
[2] I Chr. 28. 3.

Thus the prophet was more disturbed than the king, who seemingly was not upset by the denial, as can be seen from the following: "Hear me, my brethren and my people: I had in mine heart to build a house of rest for the ark of the covenant of the Lord and for the footstool of our God. But God said unto me: Thou shalt not build a house for My name, because thou hast been a man of war and hast shed blood. How be it, the Lord God of Israel chose me before all the house of my father to be king over Israel forever, for He hath chosen Judah to be the ruler, and of the house of Judah, the house of my father, and among the sons of my father He liked me to make me king over all Israel."[3]

Reading these words said by the son of Jesse in the simplicity of his heart, one may discover in them a boasting, rather than a feeling of guilt or discomposure because of the denial which had deprived him of something longed for all his life.

And soon, like a thunderbolt out of the blue, came down upon the men of spirit the story of Bathsheba, and Nathan had to bring God's word to the king.

Behold, the son of Jesse, the mighty king, in the zenith of his glory became an object of derision and disdain in the sight of his people. Nathan was distressed, disturbed, and utterly confused. He feared to go into the lion's den, into the king's palace, lest the man of blood should kill him upon hearing the fatal cry against him.

Nathan did not flee from Jerusalem, as the prophet Jonah rose and fled unto Tarshish from the presence of the Lord. Instead he secluded himself in one of the caves of Jerusalem where the treasures of the men of spirit of Israel were stored; all the written rolls, all the holy scrolls accumulated therein from generation to generation.

The book of the law was looked over by Nathan and the men of spirit who came to share with him his seclusion. Together

---

[3] I Chr. 28. 2-4.

they examined the rolls of the era of the Judges, and even to the oldest of the holy rolls, to those of Genesis, exaltedly dwelling on the awe-inspiring divine commandment of the Lord God to Noah and his sons concerning the inviolability and sacredness of man's life.

And their prophetic eyes opened to perceive the reality of the postdiluvian world, which is a world of good and evil; a world in which man is his own judge and recompenser, a world which the sons of men share with the "other camp" and in which Satan succeeded in establishing his camp firmly on two pillars; heathenism and bloodshed.

Two pillars, two evils, two wicked and entangled plagues, of which it can be said that it is impossible to tell which of them causes the other.

And God's spirit rested on the prophets, and they understood what had happened to David: There under the Satanic covering of idolatry and under the veil of bloodshed lived David, who had to shed blood abundantly. But for the Adversary it was not enough, and he deluded the son of Jesse, not only to sin against the seventh commandment, but also against the sixth.

David crossed the line of disparity between the bloods; the line that had been established by the greatest prophet in a world that lived by the sword. It was the prophet's victory over bloodshed. One should never shed innocent blood.

For this purpose six cities of refuge had to be established in the land of Israel, as it is written: "These six cities shall be a refuge, both for the children of Israel and for the stranger and for the sojourner among them; that every one that killeth any person unawares may flee thither."[4] Also: "And they shall be unto you cities for refuge from the avenger; that the manslayer die not until he stand before the congregation in judgment."[5]

---

[4]Num. 35. 15.

[5]Num. 35. 12.

Thus the prophets ceased to wonder at what they understood and knew why and how it occurred. Nathan went to David without any fear, but with pity and compassion, and he did not begin his words with rebukes.

Nathan approached the man of blood with a gentle parable about the poor man and his lamb, and when he heard David's answer and saw how greatly kindled was his anger against the rich man, only then did Nathan say, "Thou art the man," and pour out all the awful words to the king.

Now, David's answer, "I have sinned against the Lord,"[6] did not surprise the prophet; what did amaze, not only the prophet, but also the men of spirit in Jerusalem, was the deep spiritual change that took place in David; a change that was expressed so well in his psalms.

The prophets beheld how a scrupulous penitence had the power to breach David's self-confidence, his armor of righteousness, which he put on as a garment for clothing; his self-aggrandizement and self-satisfaction, which were so ecstatically depicted by him in his song "the words of which he spoke unto the Lord in the day that the Lord delivered him out of the hand of his enemies and out of the hand of Saul."[7]

The inspired prophets thus knew that the time had come for them to act. Let the kings rule over the body, so to speak, of Israel, while being constantly involved in intrigues, conspiracies and wars, but the prophets should always strive to achieve a stronghold on the hearts and souls of the house of Israel.

Behold, the people of Israel were not impressed by the godliness of their king, of whom so many times it was said that he did what was right in the sight of the Lord. They remained the same obstinate, rebellious, and uncircumcised in heart as before.

Their forwardness can be seen from how readily the people

---

[6]II Sam. 12. 13.
[7]II Sam. 22.

of Israel turned their backs on David and followed after the revolting Absalom, and also how all Israel, except the men of Judah, "...went up from after David and followed Sheba, the son of Bichri, who revolted against David."[8] It was a perilous revolt, as it is written: "And David said to Abishai: Now shall Sheba the son of Bichri do us more harm than Absalom did."[9] In short, a nation both ungovernable by their anointed kings and disobedient to the Lord God of Israel.

And the prophets of the Lord plunged valiantly into battle against their disobedient people to put away idolatry in the house of Israel.

They plunged into battle, knowing beforehand that the people would not hearken to them. The prophets of the Lord never lessened their grip on the hearts and souls of Israel, for, as has been mentioned here before, the prophets knew that their foreheads were strong against their people's foreheads, strong and harder than flint.

Thus the prophets of the Lord ceaselessly battled the disobedient people, despite the fact that the sword would devour them like a destroying lion, as we know from the first book of the Kings where it is told how, in the reign of Ahab king of Shomron, his wife Jezebel slew a multitude of the prophets of the Lord.

In Judea the status of the prophet is described by Isaiah: "I gave my back to the smiters, and my cheeks to them, that plucked off the hair; I hid not my face from shame and spitting."[10]

The prophets were woefully and bitterly struck with dismay and despair when ten tribes of Israel turned their backs on Jerusalem and went after Jeroboam to establish a new "kingdom of Israel" in which the Egyptian calf became the god.

---

[8]II Sam. 20. 2.
[9]II Sam. 20. 6.
[10]Isa. 50. 6.

Actually the degeneration of David's kingdom began in the reign of King Solomon, who was wiser than all men. And behold—how strong is the grip of the two diabolical prongs on man which work either simultaneously or alternately: When one of them loses ground in man's world, then the other increases.

David was totally impervious to any stain of heathenism, so the Satanic prong of bloodshed became stronger on him, and he was entangled in the horrible sin of shedding innocent blood.

The opposite happened to his son Solomon. He did not know war, as it is written: "But now the Lord my God has given me rest on every side, so that there is neither adversary nor evil occurrence."[11]

Therefore Satan pressed harder on the prong of heathenism in the beginning of his reign in Jerusalem. It is written: "King Solomon loved many strange women, together with the daughter of Pharaoh: women of the Moabites, Ammonites, Edomites, Zidonites, and Hittites."[12]

The result was that Solomon later became entangled in gross idolatry, as it is written: "Solomon went after Ashtoreth, the goddess of the Zidonians, and after Milcom, the abomination of the Ammonites."[13]

Moreover, David's grandson Rehoboam was the son of an Ammonitess, and he caused the breaking up of Solomon's glorious kingdom.

Of all the twenty kings of David's dynasty that reigned in Jerusalem, only three of them did that which was right in the sight of the Lord, as did their father David: Asa, Hezekiah, and Josiah. As to the rest of the kings, only a few did that which was right in the eyes of the Lord.

---

[11] I Kings 5. 4.
[12] I Kings II. 1.
[13] I Kings II. 5.

All the other kings walked in the way of the kings of Shomron, and they would even pass their sons through the fire to Molech.

Hezekiah reigned twenty-nine years in Jerusalem, and he did that which was right in the sight of the Lord, according to all that David did. In Hezekiah's reign were heard the thundering and exulting voices of the great prophets Isaiah and Micah.

They prophesied before and after the fall of the kingdom of Samaria. And in Hezekiah's reign occurred the miraculous salvation of Jerusalem, for there could be no doubt that, had Judah fallen also into the hands of Assyria, Judah's fate would be the same as that of Samaria.

The great miracle took place at the walls of the besieged Jerusalem, as it is written: "...and the Lord sent an angel, which cut off all the mighty men of valor, and the leaders and captains in the camp of the king of Assyria. So he returned with shame of face to his own land."[14] After that miracle the spirit of the triumphing prophets soared up to the divine height of the father of the prophets, to the Sinai revelations, and the prophets perceived the greatest prophet's vision of a kingdom of priests and a holy nation.

This vision was further developed by the prophets Isaiah, Micha, and the like who arrived at the universal idea of a holy mankind, of a holy world, of a world of good only, in which the sons of men "...will beat their swords into plow-shares, and their spears into scythes. Nation shall not lift up sword against nation. Neither shall they learn war any more."[15]

As to the people of Judah—even after the divine miracle—they remained as stubborn and rebellious as ever against the Lord their God, and after the death of Hezekiah his son Manasseh plunged together with his people into the mire of idolatry.

---

[14]II Chr. 32. 21.
[15]Isa. 2. 4.

Yet the inspired prophets knew that the faith in God of Abraham, Isaac, and Jacob, with which Israel had been charged at Mount Sinai, would never be extinguished.

Surely it was never extinguished in the men of spirit of Israel, and even in Egypt it was kept alive in the Levites, and then in the Calebs and Joshuas, in the judges, and finally in the prophets of the Lord.

As to the kings of the ten tribes, or of Samaria, they together with the people wallowed in the pagan mire, beginning with Jeroboam, who was anointed to rule over Israel, and ending with Hoshea, the last king of Israel, who "...sent messages to So, king of Egypt, and brought no present to the king of Assyria as he had done year by year."[16]

Therefore, "...in the ninth year of Hoshea the king of Assyria took Samaria and carried Israel away into Assyria and placed them in Halah and in Habor by the river of Gozan and in the cities of Medes."[17]

Cutting off forever the ten tribes of Israel from their land, "...the king of Assyria brought people from Babylon and from Cuthan, and from Ava and from Hamath and from Sepharvaim—and placed them in the cities of Samaria instead of the children of Israel, and they possessed Samaria and dwelt in the cities thereof."[18]

In vain did numerous prophets of the Lord try to persuade the ten tribes of Israel to return to the Lord God of Israel. Hundreds of those prophets paid with their lives for their attempt to cleanse Samaria from idolatry, ceaselessly reminding them of the Lord God of their forefathers Abraham, Isaac, and Jacob and of the signs and wonders wrought in Egypt.

Elijah, the legendary prophet of Israel, tried with the sword

---

[16]II Kings 17. 4.
[17]II Kings 17. 6.
[18]II Kings 17. 24.

to cleanse the ten tribes of paganism but to no avail, and he had to flee into Judah for his life. In Jerusalem there were some kings who would seek a prophet's instructions on how to keep God's commandments.

Actually, it should be said that in Jerusalem good and evil kings reigned as if by turn. As an example of such alternating, consider four kings: Ahaz, his son Hezekiah, Hezekiah's son Manasseh, and Manasseh's grandson Josiah.

Ahaz walked in the ways of the kings of Samaria and he even passed his son through the fire, while his son Hezekiah walked in the way of King David. But his son Manasseh was the most sinful of all the kings of Judah. For fifty-two years did Manasseh reign in Judah. And two more years for the reign of his son Amon, who walked in his father's way of the utmost wickedness in the sight of the Lord.

Finally Josiah became king of Judah, and his reign lasted thirty-one years. In his reign an event occurred which made Josiah unique and outstanding among all the kings of Judah. The event was as if an echo of Moses' outcry in the wilderness had unexpectedly reached the ears of Josiah and his people. It happened a few decades before Judah and Benjamin, the last two of the twelve tribes of Israel, were carried away into Babylonian captivity.

Behold, the book of the law, the witness against Israel, had been found by the high priest Hilkiah in the house of the Lord during the work of repairing the breaches of the house.

And the book of the law surely did witness against the Israel of Manasseh and Amon. Of Manasseh it is written that "...he built up again the high places, which Hezekiah his father had destroyed, and he reared up altars for Baal, and made a grove, as did Ahab the king of Israel, and worshipped all the host of heaven and served them. And he built altars for all the host of heaven in the house of the Lord, and in the two courts of the house of the Lord. And he made his son pass through the fire and observed times and used enchantments, and dealt with familiar spirits and wizards; he wrought much wickedness in the sight of the Lord to provoke Him to anger."[19]

Thus the book of the law witnessed in a thundering voice when Shafan the scribe read it before the king. And the king tore his clothes upon hearing all the words of the book.

"And Josiah commanded Hilkiah the priest and Ahikam and Achbar, saying: Go ye inquire of the Lord for me and for the people and for all Judah concerning the words of the book that is found. For great is the wrath of the Lord that is kindled against us, because our fathers have not harkened unto the words of this book to do according unto all that, which is written concerning us. So Hilkiah the priest and Ahikam and Achbar...went unto Huldah the prophetess, the wife of Shalum...."[20]

The result was that King Josiah cleansed not only the house of the Lord, but also Jerusalem and all the land of Judah of the pagan filth, "...and the king commanded all the people, saying: Keep the passover unto the Lord your God, as it is written in the book of the covenant. Surely there was not held such a passover from the days of the judges that judged Israel, nor in all the days of the kings of Israel, nor of the kings of Judah. But in the eighteenth year of King Josiah wherein this passover was held to the Lord in Jerusalem. Moreover the workers with familiar spirits, and the wizards and the teraphim, and the idols and all the abominations that were spied in the land of Judah and in Jerusalem did Josiah put away, that he might perform the words of the law which were written in the book that Hilkiah found in the house of the Lord. And like unto him was there no king before him, that turned to the Lord with all his heart and with all his soul, according to all the law of Moses; neither after him arose there any like him."[21]

---

[19] II Kings 21. 3-6.
[20] II Kings 22. 12-14.
[21] II Kings 23. 21-25.

Thus the book of the law found by Hilkiah in the house of the Lord testified not only against a sinful people in the days of King Josiah, but also against a stubborn and rebellious Israel for the thousand years and more that had passed since Moses brought the twelve tribes to meet the Lord their God in the wilderness of Sinai. Moses' ominous prophecies had been vindicated, and his apprehensions had not been groundless.

At this point we may again marvel at the wondrous works of the heavenly wisdom in the vineyard of the Lord of hosts. Josiah was the right king to appear in Israel in the right time. Josiah's accession to the throne brought back to Judah the godliness of his great-grandfather Hezekiah, and this after fifty-seven years of an unruly indulgence of Judah in heathenism under the rulings of Manasseh and Amon.

And Josiah's covenant was made before the Lord for all the people of Israel and in the presence of all the elders of Judah and Jerusalem and of all the men of Judah, and of all the inhabitants of Jerusalem and all the priests and the prophets and all the people from small even unto great.

"And the king stood by a pillar and made a covenant before the Lord, to walk after the Lord and to keep His commandments and His testimonies and His statutes with all their heart and all their soul, to perform the words of this covenant, that were written in this book. And all the people stood to the covenant."[22]

The vivid description of the finding of the book, together with the moving depiction of the making of the covenant, may suggest that, while all this certainly could not cause the stony hearts of the people to turn instantly into hearts of flesh that became whole with the Lord their God, yet it might have at least caused the stony hearts to crack, and with the crevices remaining open the hearts would become more open to the influence of the heavenly wisdom's good advice.

---

[22]II Kings 23. 3.

Now, when Manasseh ascended the throne there were left about a hundred years till the Babylonian bondage. For fifty-seven years Judah lived under the rule of Manasseh and his son Amon while indulging in the loathsome mire of paganism.

During the remaining fifty years Judah had five successive kings: Josiah, who reigned thirty-one years; his son Jehoahaz, three months; his second son Jehoiakim, eleven years; Jehoia-chin, three months, and finally Zedekiah, eleven years.

Of these five kings only Josiah attained a most earnest return to the Lord God of Israel on a national scale; the other four kings did that which was evil in the sight of the Lord.

The reign of the godly Josiah was like a healing sun to the people of Judah, for had not the penitential process of the making of the covenant taken place and had the ways of Manasseh and Amon persisted in Judah, then Jerusalem would have become a second Samaria, and the heavenly wisdom would have again had to deliver Israel from total annihilation in a preternatural, miraculous way. Being exposed to a century of the alternating rule of good and evil kings in Jerusalem, the men of Judah and Benjamin have had enough spiritual strength to endure the pressures and temptations of the pagan Assyrian or Babylonian environment without dissolving therein.

Thus, it should be said that in the godly reign of King Josiah Manasseh's pagan vise had been smashed, delivering Judah from its implacable clutches. And no wonder: Josiah possessed the virtuous attributes of his great-grandfather Hezekiah.

This can be learned from how carefully he attended to the repair of the breaches of the house of the Lord, but above all can it be learned from his reaction to ominous words in the book of the law.

Josiah rent his clothes upon hearing those words and sent the priest and the scribe and some of his servants unto Huldah, the prophetess, to inquire of the Lord for him, for the people, and for all Judah concerning the words of the book of the law.

Moreover, Josiah began feverishly to cleanse the whole

house of Israel of any trace of heathenism. But his son Jehoia-kim did the most sinful opposite when he heard those same words being read to him by Jehudi, as it is written:

"And it came to pass that when Jehudi had read three or four leaves, Jehoiakim cut it with the penknife and cast it into the fire that was on the hearth, until all the roll was consumed in the fire."[23]

To sum up all that had been said about Josiah's reign, it should be added that its influence extended over the reign of the four sinful kings of Judah and reached the hearts of the captive sons of Judah.

Behold, the vivid description of the finding of the Book and the moving depiction of the making of the Covenant before the Lord in the house of the Lord—all this would not suggest that the stony hearts of the gathered people instantly and miracu-lously turned into hearts of flesh that became whole with the Lord their God.

Yet it certainly caused the hearts of stone to crack at least, and with the crevices remaining open the hearts became sensi-tive and susceptible to the influence of the heavenly wisdom's good advice.

Moreover, it should be remembered that the making of the covenant took place about twenty years before the Babylonian bondage, and the awesome words of the Book that were read at the making of the covenant no doubt penetrated the cracked hearts of the assembled people of Judah, and penetrated deeply to stay in them even until the days of Ezra and Nehemiah, when the remnants of Judah and Benjamin returned to their borders.

Such was the result of Josiah's godly reign. It effectuated the deliverance of the remnant of Judah and Benjamin from the Babylonian bondage in a natural, indirect and inspirational way.

When Cyrus, the king of Persia anointed with heavenly

---

[23] Jer. 36. 23.

inspiration, proclaimed: "Who is there among you of all His people? The Lord God be with him, and let him go up"[24]—a rejoicing multitude of the captives responded to Cyrus' call, and led by Ezra and Nehemiah they went up to the land of Canaan, to the Promised Land to establish therein a kingdom of priests, in accordance with Moses' prophecy.

At this point we may again marvel at the heavenly wisdom's wondrous works in the vineyard of the Lord of hosts. The fact is that, since they had been delivered from the Egyptian bondage, the twelve Hebrew tribes had behaved themselves like "a swift dromedary traversing her ways."[25] And only the heavenly wisdom's incessant care kept them in the state of an indestructible nation. Twice were they rescued from annihilation in miraculous ways, while countless times they were rescued in natural but inspirational ways, or indirect ways.

Behold, of the heavenly wisdom is written: "...rejoicing in the habitable part of the earth, and my delights were with the sons of men."[26]

Thus whenever the tool of God's works would find in the vineyard some plants of delight which were susceptible to wisdom and understanding, those plants, those men of spirit, would become the rescuers of the Hebrew nation each time peril threatened. Such were the judges, and particularly so were the prophets, the messengers of God's word.

Oh, the prophets of the Lord, the valiant guardians, harbingers, heralds, and mouthpieces of the divine book of the law's. From generation to generation did they cry aloud unsparingly, showing the people their transgressions, and the house of Israel their sins.

They continued to do so knowing that their words fell on deaf ears and on stony hearts. Yet the prophets knew also that

---

[24]II Chr. 36. 23.
[25]Jer. 2. 23.
[26]Prov. 8. 31.

in the depth of the people's hearts, in the most inward parts of every soul of the seed of Eber, there was an indistinguishable divine spark of true faith in the Lord God of Israel, God of their forefathers Abraham, Isaac, and Jacob.

True, the prophets of the Lord knew also that the divine spark became stagnant in the hearts of the people, who remained for almost fifteen hundred years in the vise of a pagan obsession. Yet the prophets hoped that the continued echoes of their flaming words would penetrate the hearts of the stiff-necked people and cause the divine sparks to flare up with an explosive force that would shatter the stony armor of their hearts.

But lo, it did not happen so, and the prophets never got a grip on the soul, on the spirit, or on the hearts of their people. Moreover, in the eyes of the people the prophet was a fool, the man of spirit a madman.

Besides, "...the people's sword destroyed the prophets like a devouring lion." Thus the people of the house of Israel continued to traverse their ways, and they went awhoring after the Ballim and after the idols of their pagan neighbors. They even sacrificed their sons and daughters to the idols.

But soon a momentous event took place in the vineyard, an event the significance and consequences of which were known only to the heavenly wisdom. Behold, when the inspired prophet Samuel listened to the persistent request of the people and made them a king, and a royal throne had been established in the house of Israel, it intiated a period of mutual action between the kings and the prophets.

The royal ruler was the one whom the people feared and obeyed and in whose ways they walked. Thus the king became the only instrument of God's word to the people.

Now, the kingdom of Israel, the kingdom of the ten tribes, was established by king Jeroboam, who was anointed by two Egyptian calves, and all the kings of the different dynasties that ruled over Israel, over the ten tribes of Israel—all were pagan, and the result was that the ten tribes were carried away into oblivion by the Assyrians.

Not so with the kingdom of Judah and Benjamin. It was founded by King David, whose soul cleaved to the Lord God of Israel, and he established his dynasty in Judah, which lasted for about five hundred and seventy-five years and which counted twenty kings, beginning with Solomon and ending with Zedekiah.

Most of them walked in the ways of the kings of Shomron, of the kings of the ten tribes, yet there were also kings who walked in the ways of King David, and the prophets were their friends, advisors, and instructors. But even the devout kings of Judah never succeeded in tearing to pieces the dark pagan coverings spread over the house of Israel, nor in turning the people's stony hearts into hearts of flesh. Only King Josiah succeeded in tearing into pieces the Satanic pagan veil cast over the kingdom of Judah.

The poignant words of "the witness against Israel" read in the ears of all the people of Judah, from small even unto great, the horrifying words about a retribution portending imminent destruction—all this shook up the people, and their eyes opened and they saw themselves dangling in the diabolical claws of the shadowy monsters Manasseh and Ammon.

Surely they saw themselves swinging so for fifty-seven years to be hauled into the cauldron of oblivion the same way as the ten tribes of the kingdom of Israel had been carried away into dissolution by the Assyrians.

At the making of the awesome covenant by Josiah the people were shocked, and the stony, stagnating armor of their hearts cracked and fell apart, and the inspired Hebrews knew that their hearts were full of penitence.

When Jerusalem had been destroyed, the holy Temple burnt with fire and the people carried away into bondage, the long-suffering prophets and their people became one. Through the years of the bondage, the prophets sustained the spirit of the people by foretelling the return to Jerusalem.

Thus it should be said that Samuel's act of establishing a royal throne in the house of Israel had initiated not only the harmonious, mutual works of the kings with the prophets, but it also prognostigated the divine, harmonious, and conclusive covenant made by Josiah, the last godly king of Judeah.

In short, but for Josiah the pagan captives carried away into Babylon would have to be delivered in a direct, miraculous, supernatural way, as their ancestors had to be rescued from Egypt. But, while from Egypt they had to be rescued because the Pharaohs threatened them with annihilation, in Babylon they would be threatened with dissolution due to their own foolish, suicidal proclivity to dissolve among the pagans.

13

The four kings that ruled over Judah after Josiah did that which was evil in the sight of the Lord. Yet none of them reached the power of Manasseh. First, because they were limited in time. Two of them reigned only three months each. The other two reigned eleven years each, against Manasseh's reign of fifty-two years.

Second, because, after the covenant that was made by Josiah before the Lord and in the cleansed house of the Lord, the hearts of the people of Judah were charged with a pious impulse of penitence which caused them to heed the words of the prophets of the Lord.

As to the prophets themselves, they knew that the time had come for the accomplishment of the task assigned to them since the days of the father of all the prophets in the house of Israel.

They knew that their greatest work was to sustain the spirit of their people which had to go through the purifying crucible of the Babylonian bondage.

At the head of those prophets were Jeremiah and Ezekiel, particularly Jeremiah, who became involved actively in the political turmoil of Judah and Benjamin—which were caught as in a vise between Egypt and the Babylonian empire. And he became involved indirectly with Zedekiah.

It happened when, as has been mentioned before, the king Jehoiakim cast into the fire all the roll in which were written excerpts from the contents of the book of the law—dictated to a scribe by Jeremiah. And the king ordered the imprisonment of both the scribe and Jeremiah, but God hid them.

Jeremiah lived to see Josiah's grandson Jerhoiachin reigning three months in Jerusalem. Jehoiachin did that which was evil in the sight of the Lord, as his father Jehoiakim had done in the eleven years of his reign.

Yet this sinful King Jehoiachin did the right thing in the right time when Nebuchadnezzar, king of Babylon, besieged Jerusalem, as it is written: "And Jehoiachin the king of Judah went out to the king of Babylon, he and his mother and his servants and his princes.... And he carried out thence all the treasures of the house of the Lord, and the treasures of the king's house, and cut in pieces all the vessels of gold which Solomon had made in the temple of the Lord.... And he carried away all Jerusalem and all the princes and all the mighty men of valor, even ten thousand captives, and all the craftsmen and smiths.... And he carried away Jehoiachin to Babylon, and the king's mother and the king's wives...."[1]

And the king of Babylon made Zedekiah king of Judah, a king of the poorest sort for the people of Judah, and the tragedy, the final part of the tragedy of the house of Israel began.

When Zedekiah rebelled against King Nebuchadnezzar and Jerusalem was besieged by the Chaldeans, Jeremiah came out into the open. Jeopardizing his life he confronted King Zedekiah and said to him: "Thus says the Lord, the God of hosts: If thou wilt assuredly go forth unto the king of Babylon, then thy soul shall live, and this city shall not be burned with fire and thou shalt live and thine house. But if thou wilt not go forth to the king of Babylon, then shall this city be given into the hand

---

[1]II Kings 24. 12-15.

of the Chaldeans, and they shall burn it with fire, and thou shalt not escape out of their hand."[2]

What Jeremiah longed for was to save both Jerusalem and the temple of the Lord from destruction because of his unsurpassed, unequalled devotion to, and his love of, Jerusalem, the safety of the holy city became his obsession.

The prophets were with the people till the last breath of life of Judah, both with the captives who had been carried away into Babylon and with those that remained in the land of Israel. The prophets felt that they had gained the confidence of the people.

They were always with the people, sustaining their spirit and imparting them the hope that Judah would return to their border, and at their head were Jeremiah and Ezekiel.

The beginning of the realization of this hope was seen in the fact that, when Zedekiah rebelled against Babylon and was punished severely for his perjury, and Jerusalem had been destroyed and the house of the Lord burnt with fire, and many more men of Judah and Benjamin carried away into Babylon—yet, Nebuchadnezzar, king of Babylon, did not bring other people from far and strange places to dwell in Jerusalem and in other cities of Judah the way the Assyrians had done to the kingdom of the ten tribes of Israel.

Surely the heavenly wisdom's hand was in it, and, the inspired Nebuchadnezzar never intended to wipe out all of Judah and Benjamin, as it is written: "But Nebuzaradan, the captain of the guard, left of the poor of the people which had nothing in the land of Judah and gave them vineyards and fields in that day."[3]

Moreover, the king of Babylon had made Gedaliah, the son of Ahikam, governor of the land and had committed to him men and women and children, and of the poor of the land, of

---

[2]Jer. 38. 17-18.
[3]Jer. 39. 10.

them that were not carried away captive to Babylon. And Gedaliah swore unto his people, saying: "Fear not to serve the Chaldeans; dwell in the land and serve the king of Babylon, and it shall be well with you. As for me behold, I will dwell at Mizpah to serve the Chaldeans which will come unto us; but ye, gather ye wine and summer fruits and oil, and put them in your vessels and dwell in your cities that ye have taken."[4]

But apparently it was not enough. Behold, when King Nebuchadnezzar put up his sword into its sheath, there appeared Ishmael's devouring sword to complete Judah's devastation and ruin.

Ismael, an offspring of the royal seed of the house of Zedekiah, and some princes of the king together with ten more slayers were secretly sent by the king of the Ammonites to slay Gedaliah and all his entourage, including the Chaldeans that were with him.

Their purpose was to provoke to anger the Babylonian king causing him to unsheathe again his sword against Judah.

Now, Johanan and all the captains of his forces that were with him tried to overtake Ishmael and his gang and avenge the horrible bloodshed that took place at Mizpah.

When they failed to carry out the avenging, all the remnant of Judah that dwelt in the land and in the cities of Judah—men, women, and children together with Johanan and his forces that were with him—all fled into Egypt because they were afraid of the Chaldeans.

Surely they were afraid of the Chaldeans because Ishmael had slain Gedaliah, whom the king of Babylon made governor in the land, and their only hope was to entrap Ishmael and his gang and destroy them, by which action it could be expected that the Chadeans would be pacified. But when their intentions came to nothing, they fled to Egypt.

Thus the completion of Judah's devastation was not the

---

[4]Jer. 40. 9-10.

work of the Chaldeans, but by Judah's own flesh and blood, by Judah's own sons, with the result that "the hedge of the vineyard was taken away, and it was destroyed; the wall of the vineyard was broken down and it was trodden down."[5]

And a hush fell in the land of Judah; a long silence prevailed in the vineyard of the Lord of hosts, and only from time to time a voice would be heard; "lamentations and bitter weeping: Rahel weeping for her children refused to be comforted for her children, because they were not."[6] While the flaming spirit of the prophets of the Lord hovered over the devastated, silenced land, knowing and seeing that there was hope in Judah's end, that at the set time Judah and Benjamin would return to their border, to their land, which had remained waiting for them all the years.

Surely the land was waiting for them, and no other nation would dare to settle in it—neither the Moabites, Ammonites, nor the Edomites and the like, for the Chaldeans kept the land awaiting the return of the captives from their bondage to rejuvenate their kingdom.

Indeed, the Chaldeans' humane attitude towards the Hebrews did not change all through the years, and this can be seen from the fact that after thirty-seven years had passed since the captivity of Jehoiachin, king of Judah, "... Evilmerodach, king of Babylon, in the year that he began to reign did lift up the head of Jehoiachin out of prison. And he spoke kindly to him, and set his throne above the throne of the kings that were with him in Babylon. And changed his prison garments...."[7]

As to the flaming spirit of the prophets of the Lord, it was hovering not only over the land of Judah. It was hovering also over the Babylonian Empire, where the remnant of Israel was kept captive seventy years.

But was it not the same land of Ur of the Chaldees from

---

[5]Isa. 5. 5.

[6]Jer. 31. 15.

[7]II Kings 25, 27-29.

which fifteen hundred years before Abraham the Hebrew had been inspired and urged by God's word to go out of his country and from his kindred and from his father's house unto the land that God would show him?

And Abraham went unto the land of Canaan carrying with him a divine torch of the true faith in the Lord God, Creator of the Universe. And the land was promised to Abraham and to his seed after him, which means that since then the land of Canaan had become the country of Israel.

And now behold, from that same land of the Chaldeans Abraham's seed, a nation numbering about forty thousand souls that were totally weaned from heathenism—all had been inspired and urged to return to their country, to the Promised Land, to become a kingdom of priests; for the tenacious works of the prophets of the Lord God of Israel bore fruit.

And so, the house of Israel was for the second time delivered from bondage. Juxtaposing the two events, we learn that from both Egypt and Babylon the Hebrews had been freed without lifting a sword against their captors and oppressors.

But while the enormous multitude delivered from Egypt was permeated with paganism, with an inveterate idolatry, the sons of Judah and Benjamin that returned to their border included (God's) many priests, Levites, scribes, and prophets—whose mouths and hearts possessed and knew the contents of the book of the law, and who also knew how to make the people understand the readings. For the learned men "...read in the book of the law distinctly and gave the sense and caused the listeners to understand the reading."[8]

Particularly outstanding among them was Ezra the priest and scribe. He was an offspring of Aaron's fifteenth generation. As a priest of the Lord he devoted all his efforts to the building of a new Temple, the foundation of which had been soon completed, as it is written:

"But many of the priests and Levites and chief of the fathers,

---

[8]Neh. 8. 8.

who were ancient men, that had seen the first house, when the foundation of this house was laid before their eyes, wept with a loud voice, and many shouted aloud for joy. So that the people could not discern the noise of the shout of joy from the noise of the weeping of the people, for the people shouted with a loud shout, and the noise was heard afar off."[9]

Also prominent among them was Nehemiah, who was chief of king Artaxerxes' butlers. Nehemiah found favor in the sight of the king, and was sent by him for a set time unto the land of Israel, into Jerusalem to build it, to raise up its ruins, and to close up is breaches.

Upon his arrival in Jerusalem, Nehemiah plunged into feverish activity as a statesman and governor. His first action was to ward off successfully Sanbalat's and Tobiah's intrigues and attempts to thwart his restoration of Jerusalem.

Nehemiah lived to see the full restoration of the wall of Jerusalem, as it is written: "And at the dedication of the wall of Jerusalem they sought the Levites out of all their places to bring them to Jerusalem, to keep the dedication with gladness, both with thanksgivings and with singing, with cymbals, psalteries, and with harps."[10]

Beside this great success of his statesmanship, he also restored order in the social and economic life of Judah, as it is suggested in the following statement: "And the rulers of the people dwelt at Jerusalem, the rest of the people also cast lots to bring one of ten to dwell in Jerusalem, the holy city, and nine parts to dwell in other cities. And the people blessed all the men, that willingly offered themselves to dwell at Jerusalem."[11]

And so, after more than a thousand years had passed since Moses brought the twelve Hebrew tribes to meet their God at Mount Sinai, the remnant of Judah and Benjamin had found

---

[9]Ezra 3. 12-13.
[10]Neh. 12. 27.
[11]Neh. 11. 1-2.

the Lord God of Israel, of their forefathers Abraham, Isaac, and Jacob, and henceforward their hearts would be whole with the Lord God who brought them out of the land of Egypt.

True, "the people of Israel, even some of the priests and the Levites had not yet separated themselves from the people of the lands and from the Canaanites, the Hittites, the Perizzites, the Jebusites, the Ammonites, the Moabites, the Egyptians, and the Amorites, for they had taken their daughters for themselves and for their sons, so that the holy seed mingled with the people of those pagan lands."[12]

But those constituted a small fraction of the returned captives of Judah and Benjamin. Their transgressions were the last convulsions of their pagan obsession and obfuscation.

Soon they were brought to penitence by the flaming, reproachful words and adjurations of, not only Ezra and Nehemiah, but all the great majority of the congregation. And all the men that had taken strange wives sent them away, and also the children born of them were sent away.

Yet on the threshold of the kingdom of priests the remnant of Judah and Benjamin had to fight the Maccabean War, as if to prove their whole-hearted devotion to the Lord God's law. They fought against the hordes of Antiochus Epiphanes; they fought against his pagan tyranny and prevailed.

Girded with a flaming jealousy for the Lord God of Israel, the few Hebrews defeated and smote not only the many Syrian Greeks, but also the perfidious, hellenized members of the congregation of Judah, the inner enemies of the kingdom of priests.

Such were those days in which the great assembly had been set up by the efforts of Ezra and Nehemiah. It consisted of a hundred and twenty men, among whom were the last prophets—Haggai, Zechariah, and Malachi.

From the very beginning the men of the Assembly plunged

---

[12]Ezra 9. 1, 2.

into teaching the people the contents of the book of the law. They also composed a tractate consisting of six chapters called "The Sayings of the Fathers."

Actually this tract was the forerunner of other numerous tracts that were accumulated in the following centuries, both before and after the destruction of Jerusalem by the Romans.

But while the other tracts, or the Talmudic folios, are devoted to the dialectics of the thirteen logical ways in which the commandments, statutes, ordinances, and judgments of the book of the law are discussed and expounded, in "The Sayings of the Fathers" ethics are taught. And it was most appropriate that the sages, the authors of the tract, should be referred to as "the Fathers," because they provided their disciples with the basic principles of social behavior.

Surely, it was most appropriate to impart the morals of the Torah to the rejuvenated nation, which for ages was sunk in the pagan mire. Furthermore, "The Sayings of the Fathers" began with an introduction consisting of only two passages.

In most succinct words the first passage depicts the wanderings of the book of the law during a thousand years: from the times of Moses till the days of Ezra and Nehemiah. It says: "Moses received the Torah from Sinai and handed it to Joshua; Joshua to the elders; the elders to the Prophets; the Prophets handed it down to the men of the Great Assembly."

The second said three things: "Be cautious in judgment; raise up many disciples; and make a fence for the Torah." Thus the first passage speaks of the stages through which the Torah had to pass with a stubborn and rebellious people before it was handed down to the Great Assembly.

For a thousand years the Torah stayed with a nation that remained ignorant of God's law even hostile to it and ready to destroy it had it not been hidden and guarded by the men of spirit of every generation. The second passage of the introduction comprises three phrases of advice.

With these three pieces of advice the men of the Great Assembly handed down the Torah to the remnants of Judah and Benjamin that returned to their borders and were ready and willing to be taught the commandments and statutes of the Torah and to keep them.

Thus the disciples raised up by the men of the Great Assembly would in their turn raise up disciples, and so on in every generation, with the result that the house of Israel would be continually full of learners, which means that it would be full of the knowledge of God's law.

The learners of the Torah soon knew that the Fathers' advice to raise up disciples is based upon the greatest Prophet's words, which say: "This commandment which I command thee this day is not hidden from thee, neither is it far off.... But the word is very nigh unto thee: In thy mouth and in thy heart that thou mayest do it."[13]

Now, an explanation of the expression "in thy mouth" comes from the passage which says: "And thou shalt teach them thy children diligently and talk of them when thou sittest in thine house and when thou risest up."[14]

But Moses said also: "...keep therefore and do them, for this is your wisdom and your understanding in the sight of the nations, which shall hear all these statutes and say: Surely this great nation is a wise and understanding people."[15]

So the men of spirit drew wisdom and understanding from their divine heritage and they knew that the words "in thy mouth" carry a deeper and broader meaning, namely: God's word should be taught, not only "to thy children," but also to disciples, to a multitude of disciples that shall be raised up in the vineyard of the Lord of hosts.

After the Maccabean victory a period began, not only of material well-being, but also of national elation. The plain people of the land, the tillers of the soil, ate the fruit of their labor and drank the waters of their cisterns, while the nation's

---

[13]Deut. 30. 11, 14.
[14]Deut. 6. 7.
[15]Deut. 4. 6.

spirit remained elated by the cognition of "the rock that begat and formed it"[16] and also by the idea of "the rock whence it was hewn."[17] This perception naturally filled them with hope, with confidence that the kingdom of priests, the souls of which cleaved to the Lord their God with all their hearts, with all their souls and with all their might—that such a nation would enjoy all the blessings in accordance with the greatest prophet's prognostications.

Moses prophesied: "The Lord shall cause thine enemies that rise up against thee to be smitten before thy face; they shall come out against thee one way, and flee before thee seven ways."[18]

Thus their confidence in always prevailing over their enemies was based on the book of the law, which Moses ordered before he died "...to put...in the side of the ark of the covenant of the Lord your God, that it may be there for a witness against thee."[18]

And behold, this book remained such a witness for a thousand years, hovering like a flying roll over a stiff-necked and rebellious people. Yet when the remnant of Judah and Benjamin emerged from the Babylonian crucible, and the book of the law was handed down to them by the men of the great Assembly, "they ate it and swallowed it, filling their bowels with it, and it was in their mouth as honey for sweetness."[19]

Now, it could be assumed that the Hebrews would finally come to the rest and to the inheritance, as it had been promised to them, but soon their horizon darkened, and vague presentiments began to haunt them continually, presentiments of impending, troublesome events.

---

[16]Deut. 32. 18.
[17]Isa. 51. 1.
[18]Deut. 31. 26.
[19]Ezek. 3. 3.

14

The ominous shadow of Rome spread over Judah, and the tread of the fierce Roman legions was heard soon in the hills and mountains of Judah. The people were puzzled by the fact that this time evil came neither from North nor from East, but from West, from the great sea.

Actually, Judah's rulers in their time sought Rome's protection against the insidious Greeks, for the Hebrews were wearied by the endless wars, the fiendish intrigues and provocations of the Syrian Greeks. The result was that the Hebrews soon found themselves in the Roman snare.

This evoked different feelings, emotions, and ideas—factionalism among the people of Judah—which led to bloodshed between them in addition to the wars against the Romans.

Now, what the men of spirit knew for certain was that in vain would they look for the emerging of a prophet in Judah to explain the nature of the future events as had been done in the days of old.

Surely, they knew that the era of the Prophets had come to an end after they handed down the Torah to the men of the Great Assembly, to the people of Judah. At that time both the prophets and the people knew that the wanderings of the Torah had come to an end and that henceforth the Torah would live forever in the mouths and in the hearts of the peculiar people.

Cognizant thus of their high status in the thoroughly pagan world, the Hebrews faced the cunning Romans with suspicion, and at the same time with trust in the Lord their God. If the kingdom of priests had to fight again against the pagans, they certainly would smite the Romans, as the Maccabeans smote the pagan Greeks.

Indeed, the Hebrews soon became entangled in the fierce wars and battles against the mighty Romans, during hundreds of years, which ended with the Hebrews' defeat and the seeming dispossession of their land.

Thus a new era began in which the Zealots never gave up fighting, each time hoping that the victory was near, for the image of the Asmoneans' and the Maccabeans' victories and of their glorious rule over Judah remained always set before them.

Hopefully they looked to the sudden appearance of a Maccabean-like rescuer. But lo, many valiant men tried and failed. Among them there was one who convinced the most erudite learners of the congregation of Judah he was the hoped-for rescuer.

His name was Bar-Cochba, and "Cochba" is phonetically close to the Hebrew word "Cochab," which means a star. Instantly a verse from the Scripture began circulating in Judah to prove that Bar-Cochba was the hoped-for man. The verse says: "...there shall come a star out of Jacob, and a scepter shall rise out of Israel and shall smite the corners of Moab and destroy all the children of Sheth."[1]

Now, the Moabites were for ages Judah's sworn enemies and therefore Rome's best allies, so does not the verse suggest that Bar-Cochba would smite the Romans and the Moabites? When Bar-Cochba was defeated his followers and supporters called him Bar-Cozyba, a liar.

---

[1]Num. 24. 17.

Yet the Zealots did not give up fighting, for they felt that they had to fight until they defeated the Romans, and they would fight to the end, to the last man.

The Zealots knew that they fought against an enemy which came to destroy a kingdom of priests and a holy nation, and of such a war is written in the Torah: "When thou goest out to battle against thine enemies, be not afraid of them, for the Lord thy God is with thee. Let not your hearts faint; fear not and do not tremble, neither be you terrified because of them. For the Lord your God is He that goes with you to fight for you against your enemies to save you."[2]

Yet the victory remained beyond them, and the Romans soon defeated Jerusalem. The minds of the people had become confused greatly—particularly so the minds of the zealots and of all the learners.

Agonizing questions, no doubt, filled the thoughts of their hearts. And above all was the question: How did it happen that the curses, and not the blessings of the Torah, overtook a kingdom of priests and a holy nation?

And out of their unbearable anguish they sought and found a spiritual relief and refuge in Isaiah, in a passage which says: "Come my people, enter thou into thy chamber and shut thy doors about thee; hide thyself as it were for a little moment until the indignation be overpast."[3]

And so they did. The men of spirit, the erudite men became absorbed in the study of the book of the law. The cities of Judah, especially Jerusalem, became full of learning places where the learned and ingenious men would meet and reason over the divine contents of the rolls of the Torah, of the book of the law.

All this would take place in the presence of a multitude of most attentive and diligent disciples. Their flaming reasonings

---

[2]Deut. 20. 1-4.
[3]Isa. 27. 20.

and discussions could be compared only to the Prophets' fiery words.

But while the Prophets' flaming words aimed continually at cauterizing the paganism in the house of Israel, the learners' heated and fiery logical argumentations full of wisdom and understanding tried to turn into ashes the pagan Roman yoke, and thus free the spirit and enable it to flutter in the spiritual domain.

The reasonings and discussions hinged on every passage, every line, and every word of the Torah. All this "...made the Testimony bound up, and the Torah sealed among the learners",[4] among the teachers and the disciples. They lived and worked in the throes of horrible losses in lives, disastrous afflictions, and enormous material destruction.

Now, seeing the calamities that overtook the kingdom of priests, and likewise foreseeing and knowing their long and horrible Goluth, their dispersion among all nations, the heavenly wisdom summoned the greatest learners of Judah, called "Tanaim" in Hebrew, giving them the task of the fulfilment of the greatest Prophet's prophecy.

Thus the divine Mishnah was created, which provided the house of Israel with spiritual food and with stamina throughout its dispersion among all nations. And great were the Tanaim, who continually sustained the spirit of the bleeding and trampled nation.

Furthermore, seeking to come closer to the knowledge of God's word, the creators of the Mishnah immersed themselves in studying the book of the law, while introducing many new ways in which the commandments and statutes should be kept.

The result was that the Tanaim unintentionally caused a split to develop between the erudite urban dwellers and the Am-Haaretz, the plain people of the land, the tillers of the soil, for whom the knowledge of the Mishnah's rules or code was too awesome. It was exalted, they could not attain it.

---

[4]Isa. 8. 16.

With the passing of time the rift widened, deepened, and turned into an abyss full of mutual hatred of which the historian Groetz wrote the following: "The hatred between them was stronger than the hate that existed between the Hebrews and their pagan enemies."[5]

Groetz continues to say that "Rabbi Eliezer said that had it not been for the existing, necessary trade dealings between the two levels of the population, the plain people of the land, who exceeded numerically the erudite circle, would have slain all the learners."

Moreover, "Rabbi Akiva, a son of the plain people of the land, who eventually became one of the greatest Tanaim, admitted that while still living amidst his people he longed for an occasion to meet a learner alone, whom he would tear to pieces."

And the historian continues to say that the learners themselves carried, partly at least, the responsibility for the hatred that arose between them and the Am-Haaretz. Actually, the plain people were ostracized by the learners' society.

The learners never tried to enlighten them by raising disciples among the sons of the tillers of the soil. The learners would try not to touch them, since the clothes of the plain people were held to be unclean, and the learners were loath even to think of any connection by marriage.[6]

Thus it should be said that, besides creating the Mishnah, the Tanaim caused the stratification of the people of Judah, and they were the first to mark the learners' spiritual parting from the soil of the land, from the agricultural atmosphere of the Promised Land.

As to the Mishnah, its six orders in their turn were to be

---

[5]First chapter of the third volume of the Hebrew edition, 1931, by the Publishers Ahisefer-Central, Warsaw.

[6]Assuming that some learners might have attempted to stop the stratification of their people, a chapter concerning this will be added at the end of the work, in which such an attempt will be dramatized.

expounded eventually in the Babylonian dispersion by the Amoraim—the most laborious expounders of Mishnah, and their works are called "the Gemorrah." With the passing of time commentators appeared, who in their turn expounded the works of the Amoraim, and all this was included in the study of the Torah.

Such were the Tanaim, who had been summoned by the heavenly wisdom to lay the foundation of spiritual palace called "the Talmud," in which Israel would sojourn during its long, very long dispersion among all nations. But while the foundation was being laid, the Goluth was knocking already at the doors of the house of Israel.

Indeed, soon the defeated, decimated, and trampled sons of Judah were looking in despair at their devastated and desecrated land. And as they looked also at the sword, their hearts overflowed with a feeling of utmost aversion to the instrument of the awful bloodshed that had flooded the land. And they asked themselves: How would they raise up the ruins?

Would Judah not become an easy prey to the hastening, surrounding enemies? And from the depths of their hearts came an outcry: Whence comes our help? Looking this way and that way they found themselves facing the great sea, and they behold the ships that passed through its paths.

Now, watching the Hebrews' plight, the heavenly wisdom saw how they cast the loathsome sword resolutely behind their backs, while clasping and pressing to their breasts the book of the law and the divine rolls of their spiritual inheritance accumulated in Judah since the Torah had been handed down to the men of the Great Assembly.

Thus the heavenly wisdom saw how Moses' double prophecy came true: how the kingdom of priests also became a holy nation, how the Hebrews had been plunged into cruel captivity; how many of them had been carried away to triumphant Rome, and how multitudes of them had been sold into slavery throughout the cities of the vast Roman Empire—each slave being sold for a trifle—and how with the passing of time the Hebrew nation became dispersed among all nations.

All those events signified both the end of one era and the beginning of another one. Two eras in which the heavenly wisdom's double purpose was to be achieved in Man's world. Two eras, of time and similar ways in which the heavenly wisdom's double purpose was to be achieved. A divine purpose that is characterized by the following verse: "The heavenly wisdom's ways are ways of pleasantness, and all her paths are peace."[7] These divine words suggest a world in which Man would walk in the ways of pleasantness of the shining light of the true faith in the Lord God, Creator of the Universe—not in the dark, obfuscating ways of idolatry.

Likewise do these words suggest also a world in which man would walk in the paths of peace and not in paths of wars, of carnage, of shedding each other's blood. And behold, inspired by the heavenly wisdom, man would defeat the Adversary, who became so presumptuous when he succeeded in turning the thoughts of man's heart into evil, with the resulting destruction of the antediluvian world.

Thus the heavenly wisdom's achieved purpose will bring about the total destruction of the two diabolical pillars which Satan managed to erect in the postdiluvian world of good and evil in which we live now.

After destroying the evil of idolatry and bloodshed, man shall inherit and possess forever the good earth, in which he shall establish a domain of only good, in which paganism nor bloodshed shall be remembered any more, for the futility of Satan's sowing and furthering only evil in man's world shall be seen once and for all.

Now, viewing retrospectively and studying the first era, we learn that in fact it lasted for about two thousand years, or about two days by the heavenly calendar, in accordance with

---

[7]Prov. 3. 17.

the verse which says: "For a thousand years in Thy sight are but as yesterday when it is past, as a watch in the night."[8]

Actually, this era began when the inspired and enlightened Abraham, the Hebrew, emerged in a totally pagan world to become the first soul on earth to believe in the Lord God Creator of the Universe.

Abraham became the choicest vine raised in the vineyard of the Lord of hosts. A vineyard planted by the heavenly wisdom in a very fruitful hill of the land of Canaan. And the planting of the vineyard came to counteract Satan's plots against man, as has been mentioned here before.

It was planted as an experimental vineyard, in which out of the seed of Eber would come forth a prototypal nation, a nation to serve as an original pattern for all nations; a pattern of how man prevailed over evil and put away paganism and bloodshed.

Thus the archetypal Hebrew nation, like its forefather Abraham, became, in a totally pagan world, the first nation to believe in the Lord God Creator of the Universe.

And continuing to view this era retrospectively, we see how Moses molded a nation in the wilderness of Sinai; a nation consisting of a divine threefold bond: the Lord God Creator of the Universe, the Hebrew nation avouched by Him to be His peculiar people, and the land of Canaan.

Moreover, the molder of the Hebrew nation foresaw it would become a kingdom of priests and a holy nation, and this double prophecy re-echoes the heavenly wisdom's double purpose to be achieved on earth.

As a matter of fact, it should be said that the whole first era was the stage of effectuating the heavenly wisdom's divine design only in the vineyard of the Lord of hosts, while the second era was to become the stage of carrying out the same

---

[8]Ps. 90. 4.

design on a worldwide scale when all the nations shall effect the divine design.

Concluding the retrospective viewing of the first era, we learn that it ended with the fulfillment of Moses' double prophecy in the vineyard of the Lord of hosts, and likewise with the carrying out of the heavenly wisdom's divine design.

Thus it might have been expected that the prototypal Hebrew nation would live a peaceful life in the Promised Land, and none would make them afraid. We see instead how a devout and holy nation was exiled from its land and removed far from its country.

We see how it became unable to fulfill its obligations in the great and holy Temple that was built in God's name, how it became unable to keep the commandments, statutes, ordinances, and judgments of the book of the law by which it lived.

And only the heavenly wisdom knew from the beginning that, because the Hebrews had attained the status of a holy nation, of the only holy nation in the world, this same nation was designated to serve as a living pattern to the rest of the world.

For this purpose the archetypal nation was dispersed among all nations as a living witness against evil, and as a sign of man's capability to wean and cure himself from the obsessions of paganism and bloodshed, as a living pattern to all nations.

Now, the beginning of the dispersion certainly might have brought about some bitter and desperate doubts. After such horrible losses, after losing almost everything necessary, everything essential for the life of an independent nation, after all this would they hold their ground and not quail under the burden of the awful calamities and afflictions?

Would not all the curses that overtook a ruined and broken nation evoke in the hearts of the devout and holy nation a bitter feeling that they had been deserted by the Lord their God? Moreover, would all this not throw them into the depths of national and racial disintegration and decay? Yet the dispersed people were able to hold their own, their spirit remaining strong as ever.

Furthermore, the divine synthesis of the concrete and the abstract, of the material and the spiritual, which Moses added in the wilderness of Sinai to the molding of the Hebrew nation, became the most significant and effective characteristic of the Hebrews' nature, which resulted in their preferring the spiritual and the abstract over the material.

This spiritual property enabled them to endure the most horrible conditions of the Goluth, while continuing incessantly to serve the Almighty with both the learning of the Torah and with the prayers which substituted for the sacrifices of yore at the altars of the house of the Lord.

Moreover, the Hebrews continued to live in the spirit of their past life in the Promised Land, not only by thinking of it day and night, but also by constantly perusing the contents of the book of the law, which their hands never relinquished. In short, the Book became a spiritual cornucopia to the persecuted, tortured, and decimated nation, a fountain of living water that fails not.

Clad as with a cloak with the virtues of their incessant and diligent serving of the Lord their God, and with the image of the Promised Land, of Eretz-Israel, set before them continually, the Hebrews became impervious to any temptation coming from the outside.

And surely they saw and met many temptations lurking in every corner of the earth; temptations to plunge into oblivion by gradually dissolving in the mass of the people among which they sojourned, or to live up the meaning of the verse which says: "Give strong drink unto him that is ready to perish, and wine unto those that be bitter of soul,"[9] or finally many other temptations to seek intoxication.

But none of this came to pass, far from it! On the contrary,

---

[9]Prov. 31. 6.

the elated spirit of the dispersed Hebrews soared up high to perceive the shining holiness that spread over their tents, to see their habitations clean of both the pagan obfuscation and the demoniac obsession of bloodshed. And continuing to look retrospectively we realize that for almost eighteen hundred years the Hebrew nation preserved its national and spiritual integrity, preserved the wholeness of a devout and holy people.

Isolated in their ghettoes, dispersed among all nations, the Hebrews lived a life which is so dramatically depicted by Isaiah's prophetic words: "As the teil tree (the terebinth) and as an oak whose stock (stem, substance) is in them when they cast their leaves, so the holy seed shall be the substance thereof."[10]

Surely, the savage, sanguinary, and ravaging winds and storms, bursting into the holy ghettoes, would each time cause a tragic "Shalecheth," a casting of leaves (lives), yet the holy seed remained indestructible.

Their spirit soared high on wings of spiritual freedom in accordance with what is written in "The Sayings of the Fathers": "It is said: The tables are the works of God engraved, 'horoot' in Hebrew, upon the tables; read not 'horoot,' but 'hairoot,' 'freedom' in Hebrew, for man is never more free than when he serves God with occupying himself with the study of the Torah. And he who occupies himself so is elated."[11]

Such was the life of the Hebrew nation during a stretch of about eighteen hundred years till the end of the eighteenth century, when a significant change took place in Europe, and particularly in the house of Israel. It began with an emancipation trend, when the civilized states opened their doors cautiously to the immigration of the Hebrews.

The emancipation broke and eliminated some fences established for the Torah, but beside these inroads coming from the outside, there soon appeared from within the enlightenment

---

[10]Isa. 6. 13.
[11]The Sayings of the Fathers 6. 2.

movement. It not only broke fences, it breached even the traditional isolation of the ghettoes.

The result was that to the violent "shalecheth," casting of the leaves, was added the assimilation shalecheth in the house of Israel.

At this point we perceive, while intending to elaborate upon the conclusion of the first era, that almost the whole period of the second era had been devoted to the depiction of the life of the Hebrews dispersed among all nations.

This occurred because the dispersion phenomenon binds together the two eras making them one, and the era that followed the burning of the Temple and the destruction of Jerusalem by the Romans should be called the dispersion era.

Behold, the spirit of the book of God's word remained hovering over the Promised Land for fifteen hundred years, while materializing and appearing from time to time as a witness against Israel. And finally as a result of the heavenly wisdom's wondrous and divine words—both direct, miraculous, and indirect, inspirational—the sons of Judah and Benjamin became weaned from paganism, and they established a kingdom of priests in their land.

But it was not enough, for to keep God's word suggests being weaned from bloodshed, and the Hebrews were seen consequently casting behind the loathsome instrument of war, of massacre, thus becoming a devout and a holy nation. All this has been already described and elaborated here.

Now, from the beginning the heavenly wisdom knew that the devout and holy nation was destined, not only to remain in dispersion as a live witness against evil and as an original pattern to be followed by all nations, but also to remain in dispersion till all the nations went through the process of becoming weaned from the Satanic evils in the same way the Hebrews had been.

All this means that, as all the pagan nations, before becoming in their turn the arena of the heavenly wisdom's wondrous and inspirational works, waited two thousand years, or two days on the heavenly calendar, till the Hebrews became a devout and a holy nation—so were the Hebrews destined to remain in dispersion also waiting two thousand years during which all the pagan nations would also be cured, first from paganism and eventually also from bloodshed. Thus, viewing the happenings that took place from the beginning of the dispersion era to our days among all the nations of the world, we see and learn that after a few centuries went by the ancient world awoke in the shining light of the rising sun of the true faith in the Lord God, Creator of the Universe.

The inspired and enlightened nations gradually freed themselves from the evil of heathenism. And they did it the same way the archetypal nation did, namely by swallowing an overdose of the Satanic evil which aroused complete disgust.

Behold, it can be said that each nation of the ancient world in its time reached a culminating point, an apogee of paganism while trusting in a multitude of gods and goddesses, including many mythological creatures—half-human, half-beast, or fish—that filled the earth, the waters, and the atmosphere. Such a great dose of heathenism resulted in a retributory reaction. The Satanic obfuscating evil was rejected and loathed.

Continuing to look retrospectively, we should not be surprised to realize that the dispersion era is at its end, since it has lasted almost as long as the first era. Two thousand years have gone by already, suggesting that the time has come for the fulfillment of the heavenly wisdom's double design on earth, that the time has come for mankind to be fully weaned from the use of the Satanic sword.

This can be substantiated by the fact that in our twentieth century, in our time, before our eyes, so to speak, man has already swallowed an overdose of outrageous destruction of human lives, of horrible genocide, including an unheard-of, diabolical Holocaust. Yet to all appearances that evil dose has not been enough to provoke the natural process of ejecting, of vomiting the Satanic poison with a feeling of utmost disgust, the same way man weaned himself from the plague of paganism.

Thus it should be said that again, to all appearances, man is readying himself to swallow a much larger dose of the destruction of human lives. And the accumulated, lurking monsters by which man is apt to wipe out life from the face of the earth— these monsters witness against him.

Surely, they witness against man's evil genius. He is prepared to judge himself and, by an impulse of malicious hypocrisy, willing to open the gates of hellish fires invented by him, and thus to immolate himself as a whole-burnt offering, or to incinerate himself as a retributive action for his past evildoings, erasing the remembrance of mankind from under the sun.

But it shall never come to pass, for man is to be judged by both his good and evil geniuses, and the fact is that man's good genius foresaw and foretold through the mouths of the Prophets of the Lord that man will deal out to himself a retribution neither of self-immolation nor of self-incineration as a whole-burnt offering.

And thus all nations will become gradually engaged in the carrying out of the heavenly wisdom's double design on earth, while effecting the heavenly design in the same way in which the Hebrews did, by swallowing an overdose of the evil of bloodshed, a larger dose than before, and likewise reaching evil's culminating point or apogee.

All this, surely enough, suggests only one thing: that the conventional wars shall spread over all the world, as the waters cover the sea, and as it was prophesied: "...every one shall fight against his brother and every one against his neighbor; city against city and kingdom against kingdom."[12]

Also, "...and the people shall be oppressed every one by

---

[12]Isa. 19. 2.

another, and every one by his neighbor; the child shall behave himself proudly against the ancient and the base against the honorable."[13]

Thus mankind is in its last stage of being purified, weaned from the plague of bloodshed, which suggests also that the dispersion era is at its end. For behold, the Hebrews have emerged in the Promised Land. They picked up the rusty sword which they had cast behind their backs two thousand years ago, and they lifted it up in defense of their foothold in the ancient land promised to Abraham and to his seed after him.

And amidst the worldwide clang of arms, the clang of their sword will be also heard, lest their place should be wanting among all the nations of the world, whose hearts of flesh shall become so susceptible to the good genius' judgments and rebukes, "that they shall beat their swords to plow-shares and their spears to scythes; nation shall not lift up sword against nation, neither shall they learn war any more."[14]

And every nation great or small "shall dwell safely, and none shall make them afraid."[15]

---

[13]Isa. 3. 5.
[14]Isa. 2. 4.
[15]Ezek. 34. 28.

PART THREE

The Tanaim

15

There was a town renowned for its numerous learning houses in the ancient land of Judea in the days when the Romans ruled over the subdued land. A town that was a refuge for the spiritual leaders of the nation, for the scholars of Judea in those calamitous days, when blood would be shed abundantly all around while the cruel enemy thrust Israel through with his sword.

Jabneh was the name of that town. It was perched on top of a hill. A town which was then the seat of Rabban Gamaliel, one of the first generation of the famous Tanaim, who laid the foundation of the Mishnah. Jabneh was thus the center of the scholastic study of the Torah in those tragic days.

And who was it that came out of Jabneh like two dark shadows, slowly moving through the green vineyards which covered the slopes of the hill? Were they Roman legionaries who came out of their camp to trample again and again under their feet the helplessly prostrated land of Judea? No, those two figures were not legionaries but two young scholars, two disciples of Rabban Gamaliel. They were two Talmudai-Hachamim, or learned men, who had gone out in the cool hours of the morning of a spring day to meditate in the field.

One of the Talmudai-Hachamim, Azariah by name, had a black "Assyrian" beard. He was tall, broad-shouldered, soft-spoken, and amiable. Refraining from idle talk and pondering his answers, he always knew the right words to say.

His companion, Shammai by name, was thin, short, and of an irascible temper. He was nimble, quick-witted, and impulsive, and of a shrill voice. The plain people of the land he despised deeply, and he was apt to hate them even more than the Romans.

They drew near to a village which was spread out on both sides of the road and which remained unnoticed by them, so deep were the young scholars engaged in discussion. Shammai's shrill voice was heard, as he was arguing fervently.

In a loud voice he argued that he did not agree with Azariah's interpretation of a passage in the Proverbs, for he was sure that that was not what the passage wanted to say. Shammai went on arguing and saying that he had spent many days and nights musing on it until its true meaning had dawned upon him.

He continued to say that the usual interpretation of that passage was: "...but sin is a reproach to any people."[1] He argued that the words' true meaning was quite different: "...but the mercy of nations is sin." And the cruel Romans, that are cursed together with their associates, had proven it by what they had done in Judea. Even their seemingly good intentions always turned out to be ruinous wiles to make the people's lives more bitter.

He stopped walking all of a sudden and cried out in excitement: "O God to whom vengeance belongs. Let me see thy vengeance on them. Let the avenging of thy servants' blood, that is shed, be known among the nations in our sight."

And so they came to a halt, standing in the middle of the road and remaining silent for a short while only, after which they once again started to argue over the short passage.

---

[1] Prov. 14. 34.

The young scholars were clad in loose, black robes, the customary garb of scholars at that time. And it was strange to see those two black figures standing on a rural road amid the surrounding green fields and vineyards usually swarming with working men, women, and children.

But now silence was cast all over the fields and vineyards because of the heat of the day. None went out, and none came in. And it looked as if the ground was also taking its rest at noon together with its keepers.

Only those two young scholars remained standing on the road, while Shammai was gesticulating and loudly arguing with his companion, as if the learned men had left Jabneh with their minds having been set, not on meditating in the bosom of Nature, but solely on conducting a discourse at the appointed place where they were standing.

Azariah was the first who tried finally to put an end to the multitude of words when he said: "Forbear, I beseech thee, Shammai, to repeat the reproachful words. Did we not have enough of it? Besides, each of us will all the same keep to his opinion, in spite of all the arguments."

Shammai, apparently tired of his own loquacity, jumped at this suggestion and in great excitement shouted: "Surely, Azariah, we have had enough of it. But behold, brother, how great is the attraction of the Torah. Particularly when one abides, as we do continually, by God's Commandment which says: '...thou shalt meditate therein day and night.' "[2]

And Shammai continued, pointing out the fact that an explanation of one small passage of the Scriptures had caused them to forget not only the passing of the time, and also their whereabouts, but to forget even the main purpose of their coming there.

Shammai reminded Azariah of what he had heard him saying in Jabneh. "Didst thou not say to me: 'Let us go out into the

---

[2]Jos. 1. 8.

vineyards to meditate and to delight in a friendly discourse in the early hours of the morning, when a cool breeze blows from the hills, carrying in its wings the fragrance of the blossom of the fields and of the vineyards?

"Moreover, thou hadst said that thou intendest to reveal to me something which thou keepest in concealment. And now thou art shut up, and thy secret is still hidden in thee.

"Whither is thy face set now, Azariah? For what did we walk so far away from Jabneh? Was it our purpose to come here to continue the same dialectics which we practice there?"

And Shammai went on reminding his friend of the learning house waiting for them. The house of the Torah and all the students therein. Maybe all this had happened, he thought, with the providential design of letting them behold from afar the magnificent view of beloved Jabneh, an event which had never before occurred to them.

In a fresh outburst of excitement he said: "O Jabneh, the pleasant town in which the Torah dwells, and the sight of which evokes in us so many pleasurable and lofty sentiments, and among them the sweet thoughts of Naomi, the fairest amid the virgins."

Shammai cast a furtive side-glance at his companion to see what impression the name of his friend's fiancee had made upon him. But to his surprise Azariah remained quiet, hanging his head, and sunk in his thoughts, an expression of sadness on his face.

Shammai was puzzled, but without losing his animation he continued: "What happened to thee, Azariah? Why is thy countenance fallen? I beseech thee, O Azariah, gird thyself with strength and let us go back to Jabneh, where thou shalt tell me thy secret."

Shammai went on describing how pleasant it would be to walk to their beloved Jabneh while having her all the time before their eyes. How their feet would be swift in running towards the house of learning, and that they would not stumble. Nay, they would rush to Jabneh as if on the wings of the wind.

He continued to tell Azariah, how he longed to return to Jabneh, adding that even in this scorching heat he does not thirst after water, but after the learning of the Torah.

"Behold, Azariah," he said, "how good and how pleasant it is for us to be near the pillar of light, near our Rabban Gamaliel; to be among his disciples and to enjoy the revelations he makes in his ingenious expoundings of God's Law."

He continued animatedly: "And behold, Azariah, I shall not be ashamed to confess to thee that many times I would envy thy superior knowledge in the field of the dialectics applied by us in the interpretations of the words and passages of the Scriptures. Particularly when I would hear Rabban Gamaliel himself praising thee.

"But now, Azariah, I can see that thou art pressed under the weight of thy secret, as a 'cart is pressed that is full of sheaves.'[3] So, know thou, Azariah, that whatever misfortune may befall, or has already befallen thee, I shall always keep up our friendship, because never will I change our glorious and long companionship into shame."

At these words Azariah awakened from his daydreams and with a smile on his lips, looking straight into Shammai's eyes said: "Is it true that thou doest envy my superior knowledge in the studies of the Mishnah only, and that thou art not envious of me for anything else?

"Truly, Shammai, I think that each of us is apparently pressed under the weight of his own secret, and I am sure that in thy heart a secret also is hidden which disturbs thy mind greatly."

Shammai was very confused and puzzled by this sudden question, but in order to conceal his confusion he raised his voice and shouted: "What has happened again to thee, Aza-

---

[3]Am. 2. 13.

riah? Why doest thou stand here like a pillar of salt? How long shall we stay here? Wake up, Azariah, and let us return to Jabneh."

Azariah had now changed completely. His face expressed resoluteness and his voice became firm and persuasive. "Before we begin our friendly discourse, which I promised thee before leaving Jabneh, I shall reveal to thee my secret. Know thou, Shammai, that at this moment and at this place I do break off all my ties with Jabneh. And I am doing this under the pressure of my deep conviction, which has long remained dormant and pent up in my heart.

"Know thou, Shammai, my decision. Here we shall leave each other. To Jabneh thou shalt return alone. As to Naomi, I am not worried about her because I know that she will find comfort of love in thy bosom.

"Indeed, Shammai, thou mayest take her to be thy wife after thou wilt inquire at her mouth. And so, Shammai, thou shalt soon forget the sorrow of our parting, and all thy worries will become nothing."

At these words Shammai was so astonished that he became dumbfounded. They threw him into a fever, and he licked his parched lips. After a while he found his voice, and the utterly confused Shammai cried out:

"O Azariah, what didst thou mean by telling me: '...to Jabneh thou shalt go alone'? And about Naomi also thou hast said very strange words. Instead of revealing thy secret, thou hast put forth a new riddle and hast spoken a parable unto me."

He wiped his sweating face with his hand and continued: "I would rather go back to the discussion of the passage of the Proverbs, than to...."

But Azariah interrupted him and, in a suave voice full of warmth and affection, said: "I beseech thee, Shammai, do not bring up anything of the dialectics. I am fed up with it, but I will try now to explain to thee all I said before.

"I have actually already revealed to thee my secret, but thou apparently didst pay no attention to it. Now, Shammai, I implore thee, listen to me carefully, since all that I am going to tell thee is the real truth coming from the depth of my heart.

"I have decided, Shammai, to leave Jabneh and settle elsewhere, to take abode in the country, where I will plow the ground, and furrow it, where I will sow and plant. In short, I have decided to become a tiller of the soil and to eat bread in the sweat of my brow, as it is prescribed in the Torah.

"Thou, Shammai, art not only my best colleague at the house of learning, but also my best friend for so many years, since we met in childhood. And I hope that our friendship shall not come to an end at this hour of our parting.

"So, Shammai, show kindness, I pray thee, unto me, and try to explain all that thou hadst heard from me to my relatives, and to all our colleagues at the house of learning as soon as thou wilt return to Jabneh.

"Tell them, I beseech thee, that with mighty wrestlings had I wrestled with myself before I decided to do what I am going to do. And what I am going to do, Shammai, is based upon the unshakable conviction and belief that it is in the spirit of the Torah and of the Prophets.

"But particularly, try to explain all this to my foster-mother, who so devotedly brought me up after I had been bereaved of my parents in the early years of my life and who always cared for my well-being as much as she could."

Azariah continued with a sad smile on his lips: "Tell our colleagues at the house of learning that never shall I forget how by our common efforts did we plow the ground of the Torah, making deep furrows in her passages and in her words.

"Know thou, Shammai, that many times did I want to let everybody know of my intentions, and each time I would refrain from doing so because I was afraid lest I should be talked out of my plans by my folks. And then I would find myself in such a predicament, that..." He stopped short, choked with emotion.

Azariah finished his words, and behold, a great change took place now in Shammai. He was neither sullen nor confused any more. Nor was he seemingly disturbed by his friend's words. He was only greatly surprised, and even very pleasantly surprised. His mind was feverishly at work as he was trying to digest the completely unexpected tidings.

For finally it dawned upon him that his companion meant what he had said; and he was quick to learn that he was getting rid of two rivals at once, of a rival for Naomi's heart and of a rival at the house of learning.

He, Shammai, would certainly hasten his steps unto Jabneh. Yet all of a sudden his heart, overflowing with happiness, was seized by a feeling of compassion for his unlucky friend, whom he would perhaps never see again.

Whither would Azariah set his face while he, Shammai, joyfully walked towards Jabneh? But behold, was it possible that Azariah, in a sudden outburst of preposterous envy at the greatness of Rabban Gamaliel, had decided to turn his back on Jabneh?

Shammai remembered how such things would happen from time to time in Jabneh, when some very ambitious scholar would move into a new place in the hope that with time scholars and students would join him there—and thus a new place of learning, with him at its head, would be established. Yet all such attempts, remembered Shammai, would always fail, and even the memory of such scholars would be forgotten.

And again, was it still possible that Azariah had willfully chosen to follow the road to more than uncertain greatness? Was it possible that Azariah really intended to seclude himself from his friends and fellow students, and to take an abode in a new place in this neighborhood, waiting therein, until he became convinced that his aspirations to fame had disappeared like smoke?

O, the most erudite and shrewd Azariah, thought Shammai with a smile on his lips, how he tried to clothe his intentions with metaphoric expressions when he declared that he was going to till and furrow the ground; to sow and to plant. By those words beyond any doubt he meant to plow and to furrow the contents of the Torah by means of the dialectics, not knowing that all his efforts would be in vain.

All these thoughts flashed in Shammai's mind like lightning, and all of a sudden he asked himself: "Why should not I, Shammai, Azariah's best friend, try to talk him out of his intentions? Why should not I try to persuade Azariah not to turn his back on Jabneh?"

And it was now Shammai's turn to speak up in a suave voice full of warmth and compassion: "Thou hast said, Azariah, that thou intendest to leave Jabneh and to settle in the country, but didst thou consider and weigh well enough the advantages and disadvantages of thy intentions before thou wilt try to bring them into effect?

"Why shouldst thou think of leaving the house of learning, giving up the pleasures of practicing the dialectics with thy learned colleagues? Why shouldst thou think of living in seclusion, away from Jabneh, and giving up the blissful awareness of being near the beacon of light, our great Raban Gamaliel?

"Is it possible that thou hast decided to turn thy back on Jabneh, where thou hast attained the greatest success in learning, only because thou art firmly convinced that thou art able to realize thy aspirations to become a 'head' of a new place of learning?

"But what about Naomi? Is she not lovesick for thee? Dost thou not realize that her breach shall be great as the sea, and that she shall pine away for the loss of thy love?"

The last sentence Shammai pronounced in an expressionless voice while looking away from Azariah's face, and the words "she is lovesick for thee" he continued to repeat for a while in a whisper, as if speaking to himself.

Azariah answered him good-humoredly, asking him when did he say that he intended to take abode in some place where he would live in seclusion while aspiring after scholarly fame by establishing a new house of learning. No, he never said it. And he assured Shammai that he had never been envious of any of his superiors or his fellow-students.

Azariah continued: "Do not attribute to my words a meaning which is not contained in them, but rather take them in their literal sense. And the literal meaning of my words is that I have decided to live amidst the plain people of the land. To share with them the hardships and to bear their burden.

"Thou shouldest know, Shammai, that for a scholar to become a husbandman there is only one natural way: to settle in the country among the tillers of the soil, to look on them and to do likewise, but not to alienate oneself from them and to lead a life of a hermit.

"Moreover, in my decision to live amidst the plain people of the land I do pursue a twofold purpose. Not only do I want to eat bread in the sweat of my brow, as I have said before, but also to encourage and to instruct the Am-Haaretz to lead a life that should suit a people to whom Moses had said: '...ye are the children of the Lord, your God,' and as he also said: '...for thou art a holy people unto the Lord, thy God'.

"As to Naomi, of whom thou hast said that she is lovesick for me, I know very little of it, but one thing I do know for certain. Thou, Shammai, art lovesick for Naomi, and this is no secret to me.

"Therefore, let us not worry about her. She certainly will find comfort in thy lap. As to me, Shammai, my love is given to my people, to the plain people of the land, among whom I am going henceforth to live, carrying my gift to them, the precepts of the Torah."

At these words Shammai receded, as from before a snake. He was dumbfounded. It never occurred to him that Azariah would reveal to him a secret of this kind.

Now everything was forgotten: friendship, his love for

Naomi, and even his whereabouts. He felt as if "a dart had all of a sudden struck through his liver,"[4] and as if he was dealt a heavy blow, too heavy for him.

All this lasted only a short while, after which his confusion, his amazement, were gone and over. A sudden change again took place in him. He stiffened with anger.

For Shammai was now the Torah's knight, eager and ready to guard and defend her honor and glory. He put on the garments of vengeance and was clad with zeal, as a cloak.[5] He was prepared to fight the traitor who ventured to despise the Council of the Jabneh scholars.

His piercing glance was full of hatred and derision. In a voice laden with emotion he spoke slowly, but gravely and exultingly: "What didst thou say? 'Among my people I will live, amidst the plain tillers of the soil, to whom I will bring a gift, the precepts of the Torah'? How didst thou dare even to think of such a thing? Did not fear and trembling come upon thee, and did not horror overwhelm thee?

"How didst thou dare to make a breach upon Jabneh, the glorious seat of the Torah? How couldst thou dare to break with thy fellow students? Dost thou not know that thou shalt utterly fail, and that thou art already doomed to destruction?

"Thou intendest to live amidst the Am-Haaretz, among the plain people of the land with whom we are not allowed to eat. A people whose mouths know to utter only rough and indecent words, and whenever possible they are ready to terrorize us.

"Thou intendest to live among the Am-Haaretz, who presumptuously do not observe the rules of the Mishnah. They do not give heed even to the most significant statutes of the Mishnah. To live among the plain people of the land, from whom we keep away, lest our clothes should become unclean by contact.

"And so, thou intendest to give up our glorious Jabneh and

---

[4]Prv. 7. 23.
[5]Isa. 59. 17.

her numerous houses of learning, which are full of scholars. And all this thou art ready to desert for a life among the people who despise God's Law and who are repugnant to us even more than the gentiles are."

Exhausted by his long, emotional oration, Shammai suddenly gave in. He himself now became stunned by the monstrosity of his companion's intention. He was so stunned by it that it seemed to him that all he had heard from Azariah was just a preposterous and unbelievable tale. In addition it flashed through his mind that the whole story was made up by his joking friend to tease him.

Hopeful to find some support for his doubts, he began in a soft voice: "O Azariah, wilt thou not tell me that thou wast joking with me? That thou wast teasing me, while I took the bait and came out with heaping reproaches on thee?

"Or wilt thou not tell me that I fell asleep and, after having a nightmare about this, I waked out of my sleep to weary my best friend with my senseless chatter?"

And, as he intended to continue his harangue, a tired Azariah interrupted him saying: "How long wilt thou, Shammai, multiply words without knowledge and understanding?

"Thy words are very queer, and thy mind changes as quick as lightning. Behold, Shammai, now I seem to thee a traitor and deceiver, and now I seem to thee a teasing jester.

"No, Shammai, I was not joking at all when I was beseeching thee in earnest to convey to my friends and relatives all that I had told thee, putting my hope in thee, in my best friend, that thou wilt fulfill my request.

"Nor, Shammai, am I a traitor because I decided to live among the plain people of the land, whom I do not despise since they seem to me like sheep that no man takes up.

"Why doest thou hate the Am-Haaretz? Doest thou not remember what Moses said? '....but the word is very nigh unto thee: in thy mouth and in thy heart, that thou mayest do it.'[6]

---

[6]Dt. 30. 14.

"Until now, Shammai, as thou knowest, I would do that word with my mouth, occupying myself day and night with learning of the Torah, but now I have decided to do it with my heart; to do it as my heart dictates me to do.

"And my heart tells me to do that word in the true spirit of Moses' commandment, which says: '...for this commandment, which I command thee, it is not too hard for thee; neither is it far off. Neither is it hidden from thee.'

"Moses said also: '...it is not in Heaven, that thou shouldst say: Who shall go up for us to Heaven and bring it unto us, and make us hear it, that we may do it? Neither is it beyond the sea, that thou shouldst say: Who shall go over the sea for us and bring it unto us, that we may hear it, and do it?'[7] Now, Shammai, if we the Talmudai-Hachamim, the scholars—if we do know that commandment of Moses, we have to come to them and, living among them, instruct them that they should know how God's commandment is not too hard to follow.

"Is it not written that '...man does not live by bread only?'[8] So, who else should provide them with their spiritual bread if not we, the bearers and the interpreters of the Torah?

"And so, I will teach them God's Torah, which is 'perfect, and which is sure, and makes wise the simple.'[9] Indeed, Shammai, God's Law shall I plant in their hearts, as a tree of life, and this will be my best gift to them.

"For this is the only way in which to teach them God's Commandment, granted to Moses on Mount Sinai. As to the Mishnah, I will keep it for myself because she is too wonderful, too high for them, and they cannot attain unto her.

"Then the eyes of the plain people of the land shall open to see how the Torah is full of the Lord's statutes that are right and rejoice the heart. Certainly, Shammai, the plain tillers of the soil will then willingly give heed to God's Law.

---

[7]Dt. 30. 11. 12.

[8]Dt. 8. 3.

[9]Ps. 19. 7.

"Doest thou not know, that..." At that moment Azariah, carried away by his own eloquence and by a genuine impulse of friendliness, made a step forward and stretched out his hand to touch Shammai in a friendly gesture.

But Shammai retreated even further than before, and his eyes became full of hatred and contempt: "Do not touch me, because thou art already unclean. Let me alone, the mean traitor thou art. Cease to weary me with thy lies. Turn aside from me and go thy way, the way which will surely lead thee to destruction.

"Cursed art thou from among thy friends and from among thy fellow-students. Cursed art thou..."

But at these words Azariah became outraged and, losing his temper, shouted: "What hast thou said? The shallow-brained cad thou art! Flee thou to thy place before thou shalt be turned into a heap of bones." Yet Shammai had no intention of fleeing. Instead he sprung upon Azariah with clenched fists, and at that same moment a shrill voice of a lad, perched on a branch of a tree behind a hedge, was heard crying: "Hey, folks, come over here to watch a fight between two puffed-up scholars. Their shining robes will be soon reduced to tatters and they will be left naked."

The sound of the shrill voice struck the scholars like a bolt from the blue. Azariah and Shammai became dumbfounded. Instinctively they turned to the direction from which the shrill voice had come. They beheld something which they had missed before, while being involved in their heated discussion, and shame instead of rage covered their faces.

They saw that close to the road where they were standing there was a hedge consisting of tangled thorns enclosing the backyard of a house at the end of a village.

Moreover, they had not known that, since they had come to a halt in the middle of the road, they had been watched through the hedge by the eyes of many urchins who were playing there then, and the youngsters were the first to summon the owner of the house, Ashael by name, together with other curious people.

They were mostly children and women who were furtively watching the arguing scholars. They remained silent, holding their breath and unable to understand why those scholars were engaged in such a discussion.

And only when blows began to shower down did one of the lads cry out, which froze the scholars into a state of torpor, and at that same time a deafening noise burst upon their ears.

Behold, all of a sudden a crowd of alarmed and noisy men, women, and children began to force their way through the opening that was in the middle of the hedge.

The noisy and excited crowd that rushed in through the hedge began to fan out along the hedge on both sides of its opening, and faced the road in the middle of which the confused and embarrassed scholars were standing. In that opening there soon appeared Zechariah, the village elder. A very old man, tall and corpulent, with a long beard which came down over his old and faded garment. His figure was imposing and his head reminded everyone who saw him of what is said in the proverbs: "The beauty of old men is the hoary head."[10]

True, his eyes were dimmed by age and his ears were heavy, but he knew of his country's past glory, when the neighbors of Judea would heed her biddings and even pay tribute to her. He remembered the years of his youth, when Judea had not yet put her neck under the yoke of Rome.

He carried his head high. Desperation had not taken over his mind, for his heart was always full of hope that the deliverance of Judea was near.

Asahel, the owner of the homestead, was beside him. He was Zechariah's neighbor and also his best friend. Moreover, he was Zechariah's right hand in the village management as the Elder's official assistant.

Asahel's appearance was not so impressive as that of Zechariah. He was a thin little man, advanced in age but vivacious

---

[10]Prv. 16. 31.

and quick-witted. He was always well informed of what was going on in every house of the village.

Both Zechariah and Asahel were versed in the Holy Scriptures, many passages of which they knew by heart, particularly those from the books of the prophets and from the Proverbs. At their leisure time, sitting together they would grieve at the widening gulf between the learned men of Jabneh and the plain people of the land.

As the owner of the house, Asahel was among the first who came to watch the scholars, and he was the only one to understand every word of their discourse, although much of what he heard seemed to him so incredible that he would not believe his own ears.

And so, the two confused and embarrassed young scholars, their heads hung down, were facing a throng of spectators who stared at them not without animosity. Moreover, the crowd's behavior carried signs that they were eager not to miss an opportunity of inflicting punishment on the hated, haughty scholars of Jabneh.

Shammai looked like one who had fallen into a trap, and while frowning, he tried to avert his eyes from the crowd. He felt he had been stripped of his glory and pride. Scared and at the same time outraged he repeated curses inwardly.

But not so Azariah. After a short moment of confusion, he began to look at the peasants with great interest. Did he not see before him the plain people of the land? The contemptible Am-Haaretz among whom he intended to spend the rest of his life?

Here they were *en masse*, as though they came to welcome him to their community, as though they came to meet a son who had returned home after a long absence to fulfill his vow taken long ago—a vow to bring with him a wonderful gift to his people, the precepts of God's Law by which he will encourage and teach them to live.

There was silence as the crowd waited for their elder to speak up first. And he was finally heard saying to his friend in a loud voice:

"Wilt thou, Asahel, tell me what is it all about?" And ere these words had left Zechariah's lips, Asahel, who apparently was waiting for this question, began to speak excitely and in a loud voice into Zechariah's ears.

"Behold, Zechariah, there on the road are two young scholars from Jabneh. I was watching them for a long time, as they were engaged in a heated discussion, which ended in a fight.

"One of them is a ruddy young man. His name is Shammai. I heard him speaking of us very contemptuously. He is enraged at us and full of disdain because we presumptuously did not put our necks into the yoke of the rules of the Mishnah.

"He said also that the scholars try to keep away from us lest their clothes should become unclean by contact, since we, the Am-Haaretz, are entirely ignorant of the purification rules, and that in the eyes of the scholars we are reprobates.

"Moreover, he continued to pour out words like piercings of the sword against us, and he ended his speech saying that sometimes we are hated by them even more than the Romans are.

"His companion, Azariah by name, is tall and broad-shouldered. I heard him saying that he does not agree with Shammai; and from his words I learned that Azariah is going to become a help and a shield to us, the Am-Haaretz. He said that he is going to prove it by his deeds.

"I heard him saying that he intends to settle among the plain people of the land, with the purpose of becoming a tiller of the soil, to eat his bread in the sweat of his brow.

"But more than anything else he wants, I heard him saying, to teach the plain people of the land God's Law. For it is written, that 'man does not live by bread only'. Therefore, he intends to provide us with the spiritual bread. He said also that, by doing it, he would fulfill his duty to his country and to his people.

"And I heard him also saying that he does not intend to teach us the judgments of the Mishnah, but that he would teach us the word which is very nigh to everyone. A word which is very nigh to us, in our mouth, in our heart, that we may do it as Moses, the greatest of the Prophets, had said to our forefathers on Mount Sinai.

"I want to tell thee, Zechariah, before I finish my words, that had I not heard all their discussion with my own ears, and had I not seen with my own eyes how the enraged Shammai fell upon his companion with clenched fists, I would never believe all that though it be told me."

Asahel wiped his sweating face, and silence reigned in the place for a while. The crowd seemed confused and puzzled. Zechariah also remained sunk in his thoughts for a while, after which he straightened, and on his brightened face was an expression of gladness mixed with surprise.

Zechariah raised his hands and exclaimed: "Praised be God, the most High, who by His great mercy let us live up to this day to see how a scholar is come to the Am-Haaretz, not with the purpose of reproaching us, but to teach us God's word.

"Behold, there is hope now that the spirit of our people will gather strength, a thing which I have always set before me. Therefore, be this day blessed forever; the day in which my hopes will be fulfilled."

Stretching out his hand towards Azariah, he continued with tears in his eyes: "Blessed be thou, my son, who comes in the name of the Lord. Welcome under the shadow of my roof. Come near, Azariah, I pray thee, that I may kiss thee."

Azariah did so, and Zechariah embraced and kissed him. He said: "O Azariah, I have seen thy face as though I have seen the face of God.[11] Thou hast brought with thee a divine gift to the plain people of the land."

Zechariah turned to his daughter Rachel: "Hasten and make

---

[11]Gen. 33. 10.

savory food, because Azariah is our guest and he will share with us the midday meal. And now, together with Asahel, let us go forth into the fields and to the vineyards that thou, Azariah, mayest see the fruit of the tree and the increase of the land."[12]

Rachel, a fair lass whose eyes were as doves, rushed away into the backyard. Zechariah turned to the crowd saying: "Now let everyone turn and go to his work; and remember that today is the most significant and glorious of all the days of our lives."

And so the young scholars parted from each other, and the crowd left the place, leaving behind them only Shammai and Micah, Zechariah's son. For, while all the attention had been focused on Azariah, Shammai was forgotten and left to himself. But lo, he soon became prey to a pack of urchins, who surrounded him with deafening shrieks.

Indeed, they surrounded him while many of them were trying to feel with their little fingers the lustrous stuff of Shammai's robe. And all this was accompanied with the shouting of invective and curses—and even with pinching, kicking, and spitting—because the bigger lads had surely heard a little of what Asahel told Zechariah.

And who knows how Shammai would have ended at the hands of the little tormentors had not Micah come to his rescue—Micah, who was nicknamed "Samson" for his unusual strength.

For the first time in his life Micah heard and learned so much about the somewhat mysterious world of the scholars. He listened very carefully to Asahel's words. And behold, along with a strong and impulsive desire to get more acquainted with that world, an entrancing and frightening idea sprung up in him all of a sudden; an idea which surprised and overwhelmed him; a daring idea the thinking of which engulfed him entirely.

---

[12]Dt. 11. 19.

Micah was so submerged in his thoughts, which caused his heart both to throb with fear and become enlarged with joy, that the pandemonium raging round about Shammai simply did not reach his consciousness; neither did his glassy stare see anything around him.

But Shammai's desperate outcry caused him to return to reality, and as he fully recovered from his trance, he rushed upon the urchins, swinging his ox goad against them. Terror-stricken they instantly ran out of sight.

Shammai began to clean his clothes, which had become soiled with dust, and while he was boiling with rage, his face fallen, Micah was beaming with joy.

Shammai finished cleaning his clothes. He looked about more easily. He now had time to breathe. He seemed to regain his self-confidence. Did he not see yonder his beloved Jabneh and the road open before him?

To Jabneh would he run headlong, and to his fellow students would he tell what had happened to him during the day. He would tell them how the mean Azariah had hidden a snare for him and how he, Shammai, was miraculously saved from it.

All this flashed through his mind while he turned to flee to Jabneh. He should be there in good time. Was he not known to be quick of foot? But Micah, anticipating the scholar's intention, placed himself in his way with widely outstretched arms.

With a broad smile on his face, he faced Shammai. Micah was barefoot, and his clothes consisted of a long, coarse sack with two holes for the arms. With his fingers Micah tried now to feel Shammai's robe.

Shammai retreated with a jerk, shouting: "Do not touch me, thou...thou..." He stopped short, and then continued: "Thou shouldst know how to give glory to the Torah although thou hast no knowledge of her. Thou shouldst know that the Torah is like a beacon of Light."

Micah said diffidently: "Yes, I know that the Torah is like a beacon of light. I heard my father repeating it many times to us, his children. But what about thee? Who provides thee with all that luxurious clothing?"

Shammai was surprised by his answer because neither envy nor hatred was heard in it. For the first time Shammai looked up with a new interest at the giant standing before him.

To the pleasant impression made on him by Micah's words was added the pleasant impression made on him by the expression of Micah's countenance. It revealed neither rudeness nor meanness, though these two features were presumed by the scholars to be characteristic of the Am-Haaretz.

All this flashed in Shammai's mind as he was ready to answer Micah's question. "Thou shouldst know, Micah, that I belong to the learned men of Jabneh, who are renowned all over Judea.

"There are many houses of learning in Jabneh, and we weary ourselves with studying and discussing the passages and the words of the Holy Scriptures, which results in the creation of many rules and judgments by which the people should live.

"Thou shouldst also know, Micah, that the Torah exercises upon her students an irresistible influence that urges them to meditate therein day and night, and this originates in us many lofty, inspired ideas which enlighten our minds.

"The Torah thus urges us to cogitate her statutes and commandments 'when sitting in the house, when walking by the way, when lying down and when rising up'.[13]

"And so the learned man's tongue becomes whetted like a sword, while his mind becomes quick and enlightened due to the long hours spent by us in discussing the meanings of the Torah's words. And in those discussions the tongue is the only means by which the student is either defeated or triumphs.

"The wise student, or the Talmud Hacham, rejoices in the study of the Torah as 'a strong man rejoices to run his course.' True, the long and zealous studies are apt to consume the

---

[13]Ps. 19. 5.

student's strength, but on the other hand we remember what is said in the Scriptures: '...cast thy burden upon the Lord, and He will sustain thee.'[14] This passage, Micah, answers thus thy question."

Shammai concluded his long speech, with which he was seemingly pleased. Indeed, the friendly way in which he had been speaking to Micah while closely examining his face signified that Micah had already caught Shammai's eye.

Yet, all of a sudden Shammai's mood changed. His countenance fell again because in his heart some misgivings had set in. And Shammai asked himself: "Did I act wisely when I entered into a lengthy explanation of the scholars' ways of life? And to whom? To one of the hated and contemptible Am-Haaretz? Did I not profane by this the glory of the Torah? Should I not have been rather fleeing from here like a 'hind, let loose'?"[15]

Moreover, in his heart he owned up to an even greater sin; a sin which became a heavy burden, too heavy for him; a sin which caused him to look at himself as at one who lost his wits or to think of himself mockingly.

For Shammai knew that, while his mouth was pouring out eloquence, his thoughts were going astray, bringing forth an imaginary vision which showed Micah inside a house of learning in Jabneh, wherein the students had been wont to amuse themselves by teasing Micah about his ignorance of the Torah, and even indulging for their greater amusement in feigned scholarly discussions with him.

Indeed, in that imaginary vision, Shammai beheld Micah in the house of learning, which was filled with a noise of laughter and hilarity, while all the students including himself ruthlessly indulged in making a fool of Micah and pretending to treat him as a Talmud Hacham, asking him many questions, at which Micah would blink only in response.

---

[14]Ps. 55. 22.
[15]Gen. 49. 21.

Shammai could not forgive himself that blasphemous imaginary spectacle. His spirits sank very low. He even turned pale. He cast a quick glance at Micah and again lowered his head.

He was full of regret and his knees tottered. What would be his end? He realized that he was like one who comes up out of a pit only to fall later into a snare.

But not so with Micah. While Shammai was speaking to him he did not take his eyes off him. Micah became enchanted by Shammai's description of the scholars' life, and that fascination remained in him after Shammai ceased talking. Micah's face took on a resolute expression, and he knew at that moment that the bridges to his past were burnt.

At that same moment he felt that an unquenchable flame of longing for a new life had been kindled in him. And so the two faced each other: Micah full of self-confidence and Shammai a forlorn wretch who in his own eyes had become a vile and despised creature.

Micah was so enraptured, so delighted with his visions, that he did not even notice the change in Shammai's mood. He grasped Shammai's hands and cried out:

"Teach me the Torah, Shammai. Teach me the whole Torah because I want to become a Talmud-Hacham, a wise student, like thee." The pent-up longing for a new life that was as a burning fire in his bones now erupted in his exclamations.

And Micah continued in a jubilant voice: "Teach me the Torah, Shammai. Thou shouldest not worry over my strength, which may be consumed by my arduous studies. No worry at all, Shammai. Let the Torah consume as much of my strength as she wants, and there shall still remain a great part of it for my own use."

Micah's words produced such a horrifying effect on the miserable Shammai that he almost lost his senses. But soon he recovered from his shock and longed for one thing only, to flee from the terrible place.

By a superhuman effort he freed himself from Micah's hands, and away he darted as from an apparition. This time Micah did not stop him. And although Shammai was running as fast as possible, Micah very soon overtook him.

And so they were seen running at full speed in the direction of Jabneh, and both were heard shouting at the top of their voices. But while Micah's voice sounded jubilant, Shammai's was a distressful wail.

From afar Micah's voice was heard as he shouted: "As thou liveth and as thy soul liveth, thou better teach me the Torah. Teach me Torah day and night, or else thou shalt come to a very bitter end."

Soon they were out of sight, when they turned aside along a path winding through the vineyards. Their voices too were not heard any more, and only the marks of their footsteps could be seen on the road. And silence finally set in around the place.